Your Slice of Panama Paradise

How to Buy Property in Panama with Confidence & Ease

Even during the coronavirus pandemic

»» ———————— ««

Betsy Czark

Disclaimer: The information in this guide is provided in good faith and is accurate to the best of Betsy Czark's understanding. However Betsy Czark makes no representation or warranty of any kind, express or implied, regarding the accuracy, adequacy, validity, reliability, availability or completeness of any information found in this guide or found via linking URLs. Please confirm all legal and tax information in this guide with your lawyer and/or accountant.

ISBN: 978-1-7346982-0-6

Cover design: TrafficBeetle

CONTENTS

Overview 1

Before You Look for Property 10

About Titled Property 22

Right of Possession Property 28

About Real Estate Agents... 38

Do You Need A Lawyer 55

Pros & Cons of Panama Corporations 62

Benefits & Development Costs of Lots 78

Financing Your Purchase 99

Before You Make an Offer.. 118

Real Estate Related Taxes.. 135

Translations, Contracts & Payment Methods............ 149

6 Steps to Buy Titled Property................................... 156

How to Buy ROP Property 172

Not in Panama? How to Buy 188

9 Steps to Protect Your Real Estate Investment..... 202

Frequently Asked Questions 209

Appendix.. 228

How To Pay Your Property Taxes in Panama 229

US Taxes & Panama Real Estate 234

Brief History - Land Ownership in Panama 259

About the Author 265

Overview

»» ————————————— ««

It is scary. Buying property in a foreign country is full of unknowns. Your head swirls with questions:

- Is it legal for a foreigner to buy property in Panama?
- Who can I trust?
- How do I actually buy a property in Panama?

- Where in Panama do I want to invest?

Never fear! My husband, Reyn Vayda, and I, Betsy Czark, have invested in Panama property for the last 13 years. I am happy to guide you through what might at first seem like an overwhelming process of buying property in Panama. In the end, you will discover it is actually quite easy and straightforward.

Panama is a beautiful place to live with many exciting real estate opportunities. So let me congratulate you as you embark on your journey to buy property in Panama.

Easy Process & Strong Property Rights

Buying property in Panama is very similar to buying property in the US or Canada.

Importantly, you should know that foreigners enjoy the same strong property rights as Panamanians - with the added bonus that Panama encourages long-term foreign investment. Furthermore, Panama backs up that encouragement with over a dozen enforceable laws designed specifically to protect foreign investors.

Flexible Mind-Set Is Helpful

Although the property purchasing process is relatively easy, there will be some challenges. For instance, all the purchase-related documents will be in Spanish. In addition, each step of the process will take longer than you think that it should.

These challenges will be met more happily if you are open-minded and flexible. This is essential. Not only will a flexible mindset make the buying process more enjoyable, but making the necessary effort to bend, rather than resist, is also the key to living a happy life in Panama.

Property to Fit Most Budgets & Desires

Panama has miles of coastline on both the Caribbean and the Pacific oceans. This allows you tremendous choice from a wide range of tropical beach properties. If you are not a beach person, you will find that Panama also has an abundance of more temperate hill locations, some remote and some just outside of Panama City.

Panama properties also run the gamut from cities (large and small), towns, villages, planned & gated communities to remote rural locations. Thus, you can easily discover your perfect Panama property, whether that is a luxurious high-rise condo, a beachfront cottage, mountain retreat, jungle cabin, or even your own cattle ranch or coffee estate.

And this diversity also applies to a wide range of prices. Obviously, property in Panama City and other more urban areas is more expensive. However, the small towns and more remote locations in Panama are priced much more affordably. As in other countries, you might even discover an undervalued gem in even the most luxurious locations in Panama.

2 Classes of Property

In Panama, there are two main legal definitions of property available for purchase: Tilted and Right of Possession.

1. **Titled property.** Almost all property in North America is titled property. This is not the case in Panama. One advantage of titled property is that you can easily discover more about the property on Panama's Public Registry. Conveniently, you can

access this property information via the Public Registry's online portal.

2. **Rights of Possession (ROP) property.** Almost all property in Panama is ROP. What this means is that the Panamanian government owns the property's title. Regardless, you can buy ROP land and do whatever you would like with it. In fact, ROP property has been bought and sold in this way for generations. Before you buy an ROP property you, or your lawyer, will need to spend extra time to perform due diligence than is required for a titled property. Happily, ROP property owners have the same property rights as titled property owners.

One other difference between the 2 classes of property has to do with property taxes. Owners are required to pay property taxes on titled property, but not on ROP property. Note, the first $120,000 of your titled property's value is exempt from taxes, so you may not end up paying property tax on your titled property either, if it is valued below $120,000.

I go into much more detail about these 2 classes of property and how to purchase them later on in this guide.

Only 2 Purchase Restrictions

There are only 2 restrictions on foreigners buying real estate in Panama (*per article 121 of the Panamanian Tax Code*).

Foreigners cannot buy:

- Property located less than 10 kilometers (6 miles) from the border. To learn more about this, go to this guide's FAQs chapter, "What Is The 10k Rule?".

- Some island property. There are various exceptions and exclusions. In areas like Bocas del Toro, some island land can only be owned through limited and complicated exceptions. It is best to consult a lawyer if you plan on buying island property.

These purchase restrictions also apply to Panamanian corporations with foreign ownership. That means these restrictions also apply to a Panamanian corporation, if you (or any foreigner) is on the board or a shareholder of that corporation.

Beach Access

All beaches in Panama are required to provide public access. This means you can take a walk for as long, and as far, as you want on the beaches of Panama. You should never be blocked during your beach walk by a private property/no trespassing sign.

It also means you cannot build anything on the first 20 meters from the median high tide mark, that is, unless you obtain a concession from the government. This applies to any improvement, from a small pier to entire home on stilts situated over the water. For more information, go to go to this guide's FAQs chapter, "What Is A Concession?".

Post-Coronavirus

Good news. Although, at the time of this writing (4/12/20), Panama is in total quarentine, it is still possible to buy and sell land in Panama.

This is because lawyers can and are still writing purchase agreements; at least some public notaries remain open, some are online; and the public registry is accessible online. In effect, the purchase process can occur online and/or by mail.

Keep in mind, Panama's total quarantine is not a permanent situation. Panama response to the pandemic has been swift and comprehensive. It is expected that the quarentine will be slowly lifted over the course of the next 2 months or so.

The news that you can still buy property during the quarentine is most applicable to people who have already decided to buy a specific property. They simply want to buy it now.

However, it also demonstrates that even after the quarentine, you are able to buy property in Panama remotely. I want to emphasis you should always visit a property before purchasing it. As I mention elsewhere, you should spend sufificent time visiting an area before buying a property.

Keep your eyes out for the words *"Post-Coronavirus"*, in grey and italics, in relevant chapters of this guide. That is where you will find more details on buying Panama property post-coronavirus and particularly during Panama's total quarentine.

(I do a daily update on the coronavirus in Panama, see it using this shortlink: lynx2.co/slicecvid)

Keep Reading to Learn More

So far I have only shared a quick snapshot of real estate in Panama. Keep reading to find out everything you need to know to successfully buy property in Panama.

Chapter 1

Before You Look for Property

»» ———————————— ««

Things To Do
BEFORE Your
Property Search

Before I delve into all the details on how to buy property in Panama, let's take a giant step back.

First, take your time. There are plenty of properties available. Don't feel pressured to make a hasty decision. Just as in the US or Canada, there are fast-talking, high-pressure salespeople in Panama. Although, these sales people are more likely to be informal sales people such as taxi drivers, rather than licensed realtors.

Where, What, When & How Much

Before you take a deep dive into a property search, you need to know exactly what you are looking to buy. Take a good look at your needs and determine what you consider non-negotiable considerations. If you have a clear picture of your ideal property, your search will be faster, more fun, and ultimately more successful.

Specifically, you need to determine the where, what, when, and how much for your ideal property. Consider the following questions in order to get a clearer picture of your property goals in Panama.

Where in Panama?

Panama is a small country. However, it will save you time and money if you start by narrowing down where in Panama you would like to live. This basic step will save you a lot of time and expense.

Here are some questions to help you narrow down your location options:

- *Do you want to live at the beach or in the hills?* In other words, what type of climate and setting appeals to you?

- *If you choose the beach, do you want beachfront property or a property near the beach?* If near, what do you consider near? A 3 minute stroll, a 10 minute drive, or some other standard?

- *Do you want to live in a place with a sizable expat community?* or do you want the opposite? or somewhere in-between?

- *Do you want to live near services?* If so, what does that mean to you? A short stroll to a coffee shop, 5 minute drive from a supermarket, or a 15 minute drive to a hardware store?

- *Do you want to live near an airport?* If so, is a domestic hub airport (e.g., in David) sufficient or do you want to be near Panama City's international airport?

- *Do you want to live in or near Panama City?* For some people, living near a major international airport, the best health care facilities, and the various entertainment venues and services a big city provides is essential. If this is true for you, keep in mind that there are a number of hill and beach areas in or near Panama City as well.

- *Is living near good health care important to you?* If so, avoid places far from the bigger urban areas. The more remote and rural an area is, the fewer health services. A few health-care rich options would be near David, Santiago, or Panama City. On a related issue is it important for you to have English-speaking doctors nearby?

- *Are ample shopping options a consideration?* If you like to shop, you might want to consider bigger towns such as David, Santiago, or even Panama City. Smaller communities will have shops, but not a wide variety of them.

- *Is fast Internet important to you? Do you need it for work?* If so, you need to find out about the Internet providers, speed, and cost in the areas you are considering. Be realistic, the Internet will go out from time to time. But some providers, or micro-areas, are hit more often than others. Know these areas or providers and avoid them, or plan to mitigate any outages, if you can. Another Internet-related factor is electrical outages, so make sure to ask about those as well. Remember, you can always get a generator if it is an issue for the area you want to live in.

- *What activities do you want available to you?*

  o **Water sports, like surfing, standup-paddle boarding, or kayaking?** If surfing is what you want, do you want world-class waves such as Santa Catalina, or will you be happy with "old man surf", as my husband fondly refers to the surf in our town of Puerto Armuelles, or something in between?

  o **Fishing?** If so, do you prefer lake, river or ocean (surf-casting/trolling or casting from a boat)?

  o **Bird watching, Golfing, Hiking, or Biking?**

  o **Theater or live music events?**

  o **Volunteer opportunities?**

  o **Regular expat get togethers?**

○ Work opportunities or availability of business ventures?

Make sure the place you are exploring offers the types of activities you enjoy.

Visit Panama

Once you narrow down which part(s) of Panama you'd like to consider calling home, you need to visit that area. Online research is a very good tool. However, exploring a place in person is the real test of whether you will be happy living there.

Keep in mind, it takes time to get a good sense of any place that arouses your curiosity. You need to explore and get to know an area. To help you do that, I suggest you consider doing the following during your visit

Things To Do During Your Panama Visit

- Get to know some of the locals and expats in the area
- Explore the places you'll eat and shop
- Discover what activities the area has to offer

- Find out what it's like in the different seasons: rainy and dry

- Figure out how you're likely to spend your time there

- Picture yourself living there: What will your daily life look like?

What Is Your Ideal Type of Property?

Now that you have a better idea of where you want to live in Panama, it is time to clarify what your ideal property looks like. Again, you will more quickly find your perfect property if you are crystal clear about your most important property criteria.

Start by asking yourself these questions:

- Why do you want to buy property in Panama? Your answer will help determine what type of property you are looking to buy. For instance, is your purchase for:
  o Investment
  o Primary home
  o Rental property/income?

- **What are your ideal property attributes?** For instance, do you want: Beachfront, near the beach, in the cooler highlands, a multi-acre property or a smaller lot, in-town or near-services, which services are important to have nearby, or do you want a remote location.

- **Do you want a building lot where you can build your dream house**?

- **Would you prefer a ready-to-move-in house? or a house to remodel?** If you want a house, what features do you want the house to have?

- **Are you happy to buy ROP property to save money, maybe titling it yourself in the future**? Or do you only want to buy already titled property? Keep in mind, if you want to get a mortgage or use a property purchase to qualify for a residency visa, only a titled property qualifies.

- **What are your 'non-negotiables'?** That is, what attributes must the property offer for you to live contentedly there for many years?

Once you are clear on your criteria of your ideal property, you can assess if the property you just fell in love with is really "the one". You don't want to buy a property only to find out that you were blind to the fact it did not meet a critical requirement on your list of non-negotiables.

When?

Do you have a timeline for when you want to move to Panama? Ideally, you should start your research well before that date. Although you may find your perfect property right away, it often takes time to find a place that resonates with you. And as you will see in the task list below, you need to do more than simply locate your ideal property.

When creating your timeline, factor in these tasks

1. Research locations
2. Visit the place(s) you are interested in
3. Spend sufficient time in your chosen spot before you buy

4. Timing of finances: Do you need to sell your home, explore financing options, or perform other money-generating actions in order to purchase a Panama property? When do such actions need to occur?

5. Potentially, select a real estate agent. *(See Ch 4)*

6. Search for & visit your ideal property

7. Hire a lawyer. (See Ch 5)

8. Purchase property

9. Obtain your residence visa(s)

10. Get a Panama driver's license and bank account

11. Build or remodel your new home, if applicable

12. Move to Panama. Decide if you will ship your household furnishings or buy them in Panama, and more. *(I invite you to use my Move To Panama Checklist on my website. Use this shortlink: lynx2.co/slicecklist)*

These tasks don't have to be done sequentially; you can do some of them concurrently. And of course, some of them can happen after you purchase your property.

It All Takes Longer Than You Think

Keep in mind that these tasks may take longer than you think. Not only are they unfamiliar tasks, but everything in Panama takes longer than most North Americans anticipate.

How Much $?

Do you have a ballpark figure of what you can afford? Based on your finances, how much can you afford to spend on a property?

Do you need to sell your home or business before you can buy property in Panama?

Do you want, or prefer, to take out a loan or other financing tool? If so, you can explore some financing options by referring to Chaper 8, Financing Your Purchase.

Final Words

You need to do your homework. Be clear about where and what you are looking for. Then explore the community and property to make sure it is what you want.

Consider the wisdom of renting before you buy. This allows you to fully discover if the weather, the community, and/or the lifestyle of your selected location are right for you.

Chapter 2

About Titled Property

»» ———————— ««

About Titled Property

As I've mentioned, Panama property is classified into 2 main legal categories.

- Titled Land
- Rights of Possession Land (aka ROP, or, in Spanish, Derecho Posesorio)

In this chapter you will discover more about titled property in Panama. You are probably familiar with titled property. As I have mentioned, almost all property in North America is titled property. This is not the case in Panama. By far, the most common property available for purchase in Panama is ROP.

Public Registry

In Panama, titled property is easier to research than ROP property. It is a simpler process to discover any potential ownership or property issues. The reason for this is that all titled property sales are recorded at the Public Registry Office (Registro Publico). This makes it fairly simple to perform a preliminary due diligence on titled property. You can have your lawyer do a basic property search at the regional office of the Registro Publico.

The Public Registry provides online access to this information via registro-publico.gob.pa. You will need to create an account to access the registry's information. It can take a few days for your account to be activated.

Post-Coronavirus

Thankfully, the due diligence process for titled property can still occur through the public registry's online portal. And your lawyer is still able to do that investigation.

Taxes

You will have to pay property taxes on titled property. However, the good news is that the first $120K in value is exempt from property taxes. Many Panama properties can be purchased for less than $120K, for instance all of our properties for sale cost less than that, many are significantly less.

You are also required to pay various transaction taxes when you sell titled property. For more information on these taxes and property taxes, read Chapter 10, Real Estate Related Taxes.

Maintenance & Titled Property

You will hear people stress the importance of maintenance on ROP properties, but this task is important for titled properties as well.

If someone other than you uses or occupies your titled land for 10 years in good faith (that is, they didn't know you owned it), it is legal for them to go through the process to have it titled in their own name. If they are using the property in bad faith (that is, they know you own it, but decide to ignore that fact) after 15 to 20 years they can go through the process to have it titled in their name. However, the titling process takes time, effort, and money, so this is not something that happens often.

Of course, if you haven't been checking in on or maintaining your property for 10 or 20 years, perhaps it might be reasonable for someone to assume you have abandoned it. Remember this is the tropics: grass and trees grow fast. For instance, some species of trees grow 10 feet a year or more. Without regular maintenance, after a few years your property will look like you have abandoned it.

Of course, such a loss of property can happen in the States too.

In fact, I know someone who learned that the hard way. My sister-in-law lost part of her property in Seattle because for years she had allowed a neighbor to garden a section of it. When she went to sell her home, her neighbor claimed the "garden" was their property, rather than hers. My sister-in-law fought a legal battle to keep that "garden" as part of her land, which she lost. Her neighbor is still gardening that strip. My sister-in-law ended up selling her property, minus that section. She was never reimbursed for her loss.

You can avoid this sort of loss in Panama, and in the US, by getting agreements in writing. If someone is using part, or all, of your property, even if only temporarily, you should have them sign a document stating that they are using it with your permission and have no ownership claim. Another option is to enter into a rental agreement, even if the rent is only for a nominal fee that you never collect. Any agreement should be signed in front of a Panama Public Notary. These types of agreements work well for both ROP and titled land.

How to Buy Titled Land?

I go into detail about how to buy titled land in Chapter 12 of this guide. Of course, your lawyer is your best source for information on purchasing your specific piece of titled property.

Chapter 3

Right of Possession Property

»» ———————————— ««

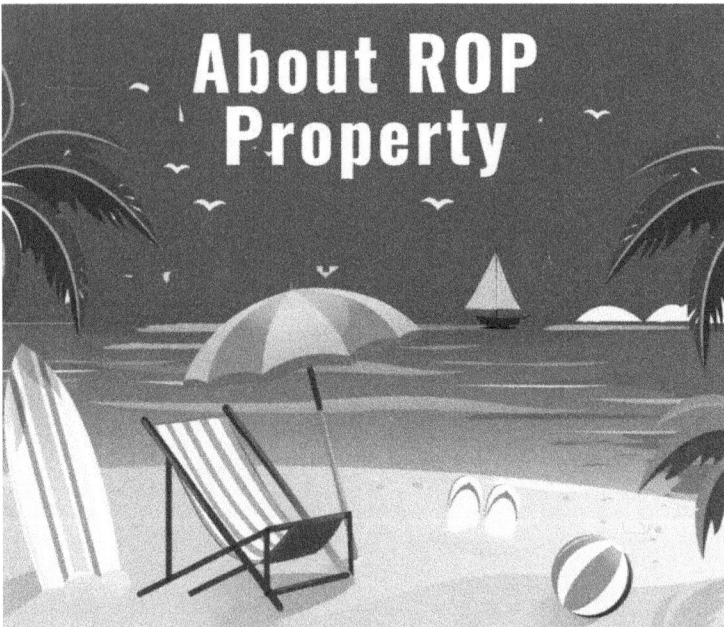

Remember, far and away the most common type of property in Panama is Right of Possession (aka ROP or Derecho Posesorio). The Panamanian government, not the ROP property's owner, owns the title of an ROP property.

Legally Recognized Ownership Rights

However, when you buy ROP land you can use it in whatever way you desire. It is yours. The Panamanian government recognizes Right of Possession property. ROP owners have the same rights as titled landholders. For instance, ROP properties can be bought and sold to third parties, including to foreigners. Most property in Panama has been bought and sold this way for generations. ROP properties can also be passed down from generation to generation, as a family estate.

4 Reasons To Buy ROP Land

There is a big market for ROP property. It is routinely bought, sold, and traded – just like titled property. You can just as easily earn a profit reselling ROP land as titled land. In fact, some people prefer ROP to titled property. Here are 4 reasons why:

1. No property, capital gains or transfer tax

2. Generally cheaper than titled land

3. You can put in the effort to title it and then potentially sell it for even more

4. Since most land in Panama is ROP, if ROP property is a no go for you, you are also eliminating some of Panama's most desirable and best-priced real estate from your property search.

Risk: Claims of Competing Ownership

Yes, there are risks to buying ROP land. The biggest risk are third-party, or conflicting, claims of ownership of the property. Happily, such claims rarely occur.

Due Diligence & ROP Property

Almost all the real estate we have bought is ROP. Some parcels we have since titled, and others we have kept as ROP. Therefore, I speak from first-hand experience when I say that, yes, you can buy ROP land safely. Most buyers of ROP property have experienced no problems. But you must take precautions.

The way to eliminate risks associated with this type of real estate purchase is to do your due diligence by thoroughly researching the ownership rights of the seller.

Due Diligence Steps

Below are the main elements of due diligence for ROP property. You can learn about the steps in more detail in Chapter 13: How To Buy ROP Property.

- **Review ownership documents & records.** Often a review of the ownership of a ROP property is clear-cut with no potential conflicts. However, there may be conflicting claims to the property, involving multiple parties or even several generations of family members. In many cases, these conflicts can be resolved before the purchase. However, if they cannot, you should not buy the property even if the price is a steal and you love the property.

- **Talk to neighbors.** Ask them who owns the property. If they all agree that the purported owner is the sole owner, which is a very good sign.

- **Review the survey of property and be clear about the boundaries.** If a survey of the property has not been done, you should have one done before buying the property.

Resolving any of these potential issues is absolutely essential before you purchase an ROP property. Your lawyer or agent can help you with the due diligence. If you have any doubts about conflicting ownership claims, just walk away from the deal.

Post-Coronavirus

Surveryors are not considered essential workers. Therefore, during Panama's total quarentine, surveyors cannot legally work. Hopefully, they will be able to safely start working again soon.

Potential competing ownership claim

One red flag of a potential competing ownership claim is if the previous owner was a parent of the seller. In that case, you need to follow the ownership paper trail carefully. This is because if a parent (and property owner) has died without a will, by law the property is automatically the shared property of all the deceased parent's living offspring. Keep in mind, that dying without a will is the norm, not the exception, in Panama.

Panamanian families, particularly families in which the siblings are now middle-aged, are often quite large: 6, 8, 10 siblings. Each of those siblings may have an equal claim to the family property.

However, when an expat buyer arrives to look at a property, the people living there may claim to be the sole owners of the property. They may say, "my mom always wanted me to own the house". You or your lawyer need to ask to see the paperwork that supports that claim.

Even if there is no paperwork, it is not uncommon for the other family members to happily grant ownership to the sibling that currently resides in the house. If so, you need to get each sibling to sign a document to that effect. Or if they all want to share in the proceeds of the sale, then each sibling must also sign the sale contract. If all family members can't agree to sell the property, now is your chance to run away as fast as you can from the sale.

A Post-Purchase Ownership Claim

In the unlikely case that a competing ownership claim does occur, it usually arises within the first few weeks after a property changes hands. When this happens, it is almost always a result of a too-quick purchase without a thorough investigation.

If there are additional owners of the property, they may claim that the sale is void, since they did not sign off on it. Or they may demand additional payment from you, the buyer. If their claims are weak, they might accept $100, $200 or $500 in cash in exchange for signing over their ownership rights. However, if they have a strong claim and, especially if they are well connected, you may be in for a long legal battle.

Due Diligence Team

If you have a good lawyer or real estate agent this process will be much easier. Your lawyer or real estate agent can do all the necessary due diligence on the property you're considering. In the case of some properties, a local lawyer or agent may have already done all the necessary research.

Mortgage & Visa Considerations

If you plan on financing your property purchase with a local bank mortgage, you cannot buy ROP property.

Banks will only finance titled properties. Likewise, if you plan on using your property purchase to qualify for a residency visa, you must buy a titled property.

How To Buy ROP – Without All That Work

If you want to skip the need to investigate and still buy ROP, you can safely do so by buying from someone, like my husband and me, who have done all that investigatory work for you.

Of course, you should still have your lawyer review the documents and history of ownership of the property. However, if a reliable person has already gathered all the documents and done a thorough investigation, this will save you both time and money. You can ask them to simply share those documents with you.

My husband and I are an example of sellers with pre-vetted properties. If you like Puerto Armuelles, you should explore our properties by using this shortlink: lynx2.co/sliceliprop.

Post-Coronavirus

While Panama's quarentine is in effect, a comprehensive ROP due diligence process will be more time-consuming to complete. Given social distancing and the very limited time people are allowed to leave their homes, it will be hard to contact neighbors in person. You may want to ask them for their cell phone numbers so you can ask them about the property and it ownership over the phone

However, given these restrictions, there is a simplier, faster, and more secure option. That is, focus on property that has already been vetted, as described in the section above.

Titling ROP Land

The bulk of ROP land can be titled. Getting title to your ROP land is not hard. Be aware this is not a fast process. Generally, it takes years to title a property. If you want to find out how to title, check out my free and easy-to-follow guide, "How To Title ROP Panama Real Estate", by using this shortlink: lynx2.co/slice.

Keep in mind, if you decide to title your property, you will also need to start paying annual property taxes. Although, as I've mentioned, the first $120k of value of your primary titled Panama residence is exempt. Find out about tax exemptions in Chapter 11 of this guide.

Final Words

As you've now read, buying ROP property involves more work than buying titled property. However, for many of us it is worth it. You have the right to use ROP property in any way you want, just as if you held title to the land. Panamanian law recognizes that right.

As I mentioned above, you can also title almost all ROP properties. Given that you have already done all the necessary due diligence, you are unlikely to encounter unexpected problems during the titling process.

To learn all the ins and outs of buying ROP Property, check out Chapter 13 of this guide.

Chapter 4

About Real Estate Agents

$$\gg\!\!\!-\!\!\!-\!\!\!-\!\!\!-\!\!\!-\!\!\!\ll$$

Real Estate Agents

Real estate agents in Panama are not the same as real estate agents in North America. Licensed real estate agents are almost completely unregulated in Panama. On top of that, most agents are unlicensed.

That said, it is still a good idea to use a realtor in Panama. This is primarily because, without an agent, it is almost impossible to learn about all the property for sale in an area. In Panama, most sellers never list their properties online, especially Panamanian sellers. It is all word of mouth, which is why having a reputable real estate agent is a very good idea. What's more, a good agent can help you successfully navigate the buying process. Your lawyer can help with the purchase process as well.

Later in this chapter, I will explain how to find a good realtor. However, here is a bit more about realtors in Panama, and what to watch out for.

No Code of Ethics for Realtors

Sadly, in Panama the bar is very low, in terms of what are considered to be honest real estate practices. In Panama, there are no legal requirements for "full disclosure" in property sales, nor is there a code of ethics for real estate agents.

Of course, that does not mean that there are no honest real estate agents. There are some excellent agents. However, don't assume that an agent is necessarily working in your interest or is regulated by the same ethics and laws that a realtor would be guided by "back home".

No Fiduciary Duty To Clients

Panamanian realtors have no legal duty to protect your interests. Again, there is no code of ethics for Panamanian real estate agents.

No MLS

There's no multiple listing service (MLS) in Panama. Well, one does exist but the listings are quite limited and it is not used as an information-sharing portal as it is in North America.

Agent Can Work For Both Buyer & Seller

Often in Panama, the buyer's agent also represents the seller. This is something that isn't done in the States. This is because a realtor who is representing both parties has a conflict of interest.

While this isn't always a terrible situation, you should definitely be aware of it at the outset. You need to be clear about whose interests your agent is protecting. You should ask if "your" agent is going to be paid by the seller when the property is sold. Your agent needs to be clear about this.

Need To Use More Than 1 Agent

There is little or no cooperation or commission sharing among realtors. This means you will only be shown properties for which your realtor has a commission agreement worked out with the buyer in advance of a sale.

That is the most noticeable difference between the US and Panama. In the US, your agent can take you to see any property that is for sale. They can do that because there is a standardized and industry-wide agreement in place, which gives your agent a commission no matter who listed the property.

Because there is no commission sharing in Panama, your agent will only show you a property for which they have an agreement with the owner to get a commission. The property next door may also be for sale, but your agent will not mention it, if that owner hasn't already agreed to pay him or her a commission.

Exclusive Listings Not The Norm

Many properties you see for sale do not have an exclusive listing with one agent or company. Typically, the seller spreads the word that they will pay a commission to anyone who brings them a buyer. This informal notification gets around town, word-of-mouth really works in most areas of Panama.

Because of this you may encounter the same property at several different prices on various real estate websites.

Commissions

The standard real estate commission in Panama is 5% of the sale price. In some cases if the property is remotely located or requires special resources to show, such as island properties, it is common for real estate companies to charge a higher percentage to offset the expenses of showing the property.

The seller pays the commission. However, if you are an expat who is buying directly from a local, especially a Panamanian who is poor, you will be expected to pay the commission.

Agents only make money if they sell you a property, so keep that in mind when they are pressuring you to buy a property. Take what they say with a grain of salt. They definitely want you to buy now. However, you should "sleep on it", before making a decision.

Potential Scams by Dishonest Agents

There are plenty of disreputable agents in Panama, licensed and unlicensed. These are agents that fully embrace what Panama terms 'juega vivo'. Juega vivo means to take advantage of a situation in an unfair way (or scam). It is something to be aware of, and something that, with care, you can avoid.

In general, you can avoid any shady dealings by taking your time. This way you and your lawyer can carefully review the transaction history of any property you are interested in. Do not succumb to pressure to buy a property in haste. It is your money; you are in the driver's seat.

Your Agent "Flips" the Property - To You

Non-reputable agents have been known to tie up a property just before you buy it. Typically, the agent brings the buyer to look at the property. If the buyer wants to make an offer, the agent then pre-buys the property since the agent already knows he can flip it to you and make a killing.

This is a con job, although you do end up owning the property.

There are variations on this theme, but in general, the price the original seller gets is much less than what the expat buyer pays. The agent pockets the difference. And the buyer never knows that it happened. However, occasionally they do learn about it eventually.

In one case we know of, a Panamanian seller had been asking $5,000 for a property. He was desperate to sell. Then one day, we learned from the neighbors that this property had just sold for $20,000! Amazing! (Not really). When we discovered that it sold to a new-to-town expat, and which local "agent" helped broker the deal, it is quite clear what happened.

The agent most likely bought the property from the seller, (in his name, a ghost buyer, or a corporation) at the owner's asking price of $5k. Then the agent sold that property to his expat client for $20k. However, the agent implied that the client was buying the property from the original seller. The agent sold it to his expat client at a much higher price than what the agent has paid to the original seller. This whole sleight-of-hand is easy to accomplish since the ultimate expat buyer usually does not speak or read Spanish.

How to Avoid The Scam

To avoid this happening, take your time. You and your lawyer should review the property's transaction history carefully. Importantly, you should meet with the purported seller yourself, with a translator if needed, and without your realtor/property finder present.

Ask the seller about the property, if there are any co-owners, and how much he wants for the property. Make sure what the sellers tell you is the same as what your agent has been telling you. If the agent discourages you from meeting with the seller, you should not buy the property. It means they are hiding something.

Agent Continues to "Help" the Buyer

Sadly, these victims may continue to trust the "friendly" agent and even allow them to help manage a remodel or new construction project for them. In many instances, this is another opportunity for the agent to skim more money and increase his profits.

"Friend" Tactic

Obviously, the people who are most successful at this kind of fraud present themselves as the expat's friend. Generally, they are expats. They might even introduce you to a few other expats who will vouch for them. The salient trait of a good con man is the ability to appear to be someone with insider knowledge who is going to be your friend for years to come.

Smokescreen Tactic

Another tactic used by real estate agents who work in this unscrupulous way is to create a "smokescreen" (in Panama, they call this practice "throwing feathers into the fan") to disguise their dishonest business practices and to separate their prey out from others who could have warned them about the likelihood of a con job.

Character Assassination Tactic

One practice that is popular is to assassinate the character of anyone they think could tip off the prospective buyer, whether those are their real estate "competitors" or simply other expats who might also caution you to take it slow. The agent keeps you in a bubble of people who won't rock the boat for them, so "all systems are go" for a sale.

Don't Tell Tactic

Another thing that the swindlers do to delay or camouflage these scams is to warn the expat buyer, *"Whatever you do, don't tell anyone that you bought this. I don't want any of the other folks who wanted the house to be upset."* Or *"Don't tell anyone you just bought this, because we don't want anyone to know that the man/woman who sold the property has all this cash on them....they might get robbed".* These techniques are designed to isolate the buyer from those who might warn them about the purchase, until after all the payments have been made. If you are told these things, either walk away or verify the purchase before continuing.

Solutions

Again, when buying real estate through an agent, it is advisable to talk to the property owner directly. Ask them about the property, including the sales price. If the real estate agent refuses to allow this, you should walk away from the deal.

If you are sure the agent is trying to cheat you, you may decide to go back and buy the property directly from the owner. Be aware that if you do that, your agent will not like it and may talk badly about you. There is a good possibility they will claim you are cheating them, not the other way around.

As a general practice, you should not go behind your agents back and deal directly with an owner to whom your agent introduced you. Your agent is working hard for you and deserves his or her commission. However, if you know that they are actively trying to scam you, you should consider how you want to respond.

How To Find A Good Realtor

There are good real estate agents in Panama. But you need to do your due diligence before working with one.

You want to choose a real estate professional who is reputable, who understands your goals, and will help protect your interests.

Google & Reference Search

We advise you to run a Google search on a realtor to see if his or her name turns up any negative information. Of course, keep in mind that sometimes negative things are said on the Internet that have no basis in fact. However, if you read a negative opinion, this is your cue to ask around town to see if this is a widely-held opinion.

You can also ask about agents from locals as well as on Panama-related forums and Facebook groups.

Online Presence

It's also worth paying attention to how active or inactive the agent is online. Do they have a good website or work-related social media account? Is their contact information up-to-date?

Of course, it isn't essential for an agent to have an online presence. However, a strong online presence does point to an agent who is more professional and is in real estate for the long haul.

Post-Coronavirus

Working with a real estate agent who is comfortable with technolgy is even more useful and important in a post-coronavirus world. For instance, even during the quarentine, a good agent can get answers to your questions about specific properties from online sources, digitally, by mail, and/or by phone.

Also, during the quarentine, your ability to visit properties is pretty much nonexistent. Therefore, if you are still shopping for property, choosing an agent with extensive online listings and resources is very helpful.

As I mentioned, a tech-savy agent can help you vet properties remotely. On the plus side, pre-vetting or winnowing your property choices now may give you an early-bird advantage once the quarentine is lifted.

If you are ready-to-buy a specific property, a good agent can help you complete the purchase process, even during the total quarentine.

Knowledgeable, Responsive & Honest

As you consider using a real estate agent, consider the following questions and issues. Does the agent seem to know the area you are interested in? Remember, many properties are not online, most do not even have for sale signs posted. To discover all the properties for sale, your agent needs to have first-hand property information.

You should also check the knowledge and veracity of an agent by asking questions to which you already know the answers. For instance, you might ask them about a familiar neighborhood, or how to do due diligence on an ROP property. Then evaluate their answers against what you have learned from reading this guide and other sources.

Was the agent's response correct, was it clear and understandable, and did they reply in a timely manner? If they didn't know an answer, did they try to bluff you, or did they admit they did not know? You want to assess the agent's knowledge, honesty, and responsiveness.

Listens & Remembers

You need an agent who really wants to find the perfect property for you. A key ingredient is how well he or she listens to you. Does the agent repeatedly ask your name or what you are looking for?

A good sign is if the agent takes notes about what you do and don't like and then goes on to show you properties that fit your property criteria.

If you are only looking for beachfront properties and your agent repeatedly tries to interest you in non-beach properties, he is not working in your best interest.

It could be he is only showing you properties from which he earns more money or he simply doesn't have any beachfront properties in his inventory. Regardless, you are wasting your time with this agent. You should find a new one.

There is no guaranteed recipe for avoiding a useless or dishonest agent. However, if you ask questions and pay attention to your "spidey-senses" you will most likely find an agent, or agents, who will help you find your perfect property.

Have Clear Expectations

Make sure that you are clear with the realtor beforehand about what they will (or will not) do to close the deal. Some agents will simply show you the property. And that is all. They don't help you through the buying process, past getting their commission, of course. Other realtors will assist you in getting seller financing, and getting all your questions answered, and more. You should clarify your expectations before you get started. Putting these expectations in a signed contract with your agent is best.

Communication Methods

Discover how your agent likes to communicate. In general, your local real estate agent will want to make you happy. So much so they will agree to whichever communication method you suggest, even if it is one that is difficult for them to use. Therefore, ask, "what is the best way to contact you?" rather than "Can we communicate by email (or whatever)?"

Do You Need A Realtor?

You do not have to use a realtor. Many real estate transactions in Panama are done without an agent.

Your lawyer can help guide you through the purchase process, including all the paperwork. It is something lawyers often do in Panama. And though lawyers are very useful once you know what property you want to buy, they are unlikely to help you much in your search for property. At least, this has been our experience.

Instead you could ask locals and area expats about what properties are for sale and look at online listings.

In conclusion, using a knowledgeable and reputable agent will make your property search faster and provide you with more information. Plus some agents can offer you the comfort of having a strong and reliable ally in the process. This can be the case from buying from some owners as well. For instance, although we are not real estate agents, Reyn and I offer our help and support to each person who buys one of our properties.

Chapter 5

Do You Need A Lawyer

»» ———————————— ««

Lawyers in Panama

Unless you have significant experience buying property in Panama, you will want to hire a lawyer to help you. Real estate transactions can have unexpected complications. A good real estate lawyer can help you avoid such unforeseen complications.

Plus, all the paperwork is in Spanish "Legalese" which Panamanian lawyers are very familiar with.

Tips on Hiring A Lawyer

- Be sure the lawyer is not affiliated with the seller. The rules governing an attorney's ethics and conflict of interest in Panama are marginal at best.

- Ensure that your lawyer has experience in real estate transactions, not just with immigration or processing corporations.

- Be clear about what you expect your lawyer to do for you

- Get a quote up front for their services

- Put all this in writing as part of a professional services agreement

Finding a Good Lawyer

Truth be told, there are many many terrible lawyers in Panama. But there are good ones too.

What this means is you should choose carefully when hiring a lawyer.

How can you tell if your lawyer is any good?

You want to be sure you have a lawyer who is a good communicator and doesn't leave you hanging. If you ask your lawyer three questions in one email, he or she should answer all three, at least most of the time.

How to find a good lawyer

Getting recommendations for a good lawyer is the best method. However, just because that lawyer did a wonderful job for your friend, does not necessarily mean that same lawyer will do a good job for you. However, a recommendation is a good indicator of reliability, especially if a number of people have had equally good experiences with that lawyer. Keep in mind that all lawyers in a firm are not equal. If a friend recommends Lawyer Y with Firm A, Lawyer X at the same Firm A may not be nearly as good.

You can ask local expats for lawyer recommendations on forums, Whatsapp groups, Facebook groups, and other places where expats converse.

My Rule of Thumb. I have a 3-recommendation rule of thumb. That is, if a lawyer is highly recommended by at least 3 different people that lawyer is worth looking into.

Also, if someone mentions a lawyer in a forum, it is best to private message them about their experience with that lawyer. You are much more likely to learn their real opinion and experience that way. Panama has strict libel laws so people tend to keep negative comments about lawyers off public forums.

Also make sure that the lawyer you hire is well versed in real estate, not primarily immigration or another specialty.

Post-Coronavirus

As with real estate agents, in the in post-coronavirus world hiring a lawyer who is tech savvy is particularly useful and important. You want a lawyer who can complete the purchase process using online resources.

You should ask if the lawyer has access to a pulbic notary during the total quarentine. During the total quarentine, public notaries are considered essential workers. However, only some public notary offices decided to remain open. Some of these notaries are available online.

Recommended Lawyers

I have hired many lawyers in our dozen or so years in Panama. I must say he is the only lawyer I have used for real estate (and immigration) who has consistently done a good job for us. Many other people have hired him with good results as well. I am sure there are other equally good lawyers out there, however, I can only vouch one.

I don't feel comfortable putting an explicit lawyer recommendation in this guide. However, if you contact me via my website (lynx2.co/slicecontact), I'd be happy to share his name and contact info with you. The good news is that he is very tech-savy and is able to do the purchase process remotely, even during Panama's total quarantine.

What A Lawyer Does
A lawyer can help with many tasks, including:

- Review and ask for changes to the sales contract

- Assist in setting up an escrow account (or other payment option)
- Conduct a title search
- Research ROP properties
- Investigate and confirm the Property (Catastral) Value used for property taxes. Discover if there is a tax exemption on the property, and ensure it is transferred to new owner if applicable
- Review relevant documents to confirm that all real estate transaction taxes, property taxes, and outstanding utility bills are paid and in good standing. (Note: It is the seller's responsibility to pay all taxes and obtain documents showing that the property is unencumbered by liens and outstanding debts)
- Register the title once you have bought the property
- Obtain English translations of all documents

All the tasks the lawyer will do, as well as the payments expected for doing them, should be clearly stipulated in the professional services agreement.

Once again, a good lawyer can remove much of the risk and hassle from a real estate transaction in Panama.

Chapter 6

Pros & Cons of Panama Corporations

»» ———————————— ««

To Have One, Or Not

CORPORATION

A heads up, when you buy property in Panama.

Many lawyers will urge you to create a corporation first. Often this course of action is presented as the only option.

But it isn't. In the case of Americans, forming a corporation can be a big disadvantage.

You do not need to form a corporation. There's nothing to prevent you from buying a property in your own name. Foreigners and locals alike can buy property in Panama - in their own names.

Remember that a lawyer who insists you need to form a corporation, will also earn a fee when they help you create that corporation. And keep earning annually after that to keep it active, although the renewal fee is much lower.

However, there are some good reasons to hold your Panama property in a corporation. I will describe those reasons further on in this post.

The way you choose to hold your Panama property depends upon the property, your needs, as well as other considerations particular to you. There are 3 ways to hold your Panama real estate.

3 Ways to Hold Panama Property

- Under your personal name

- In the name of a Panamanian corporation
- In the name of a Private Interest Foundation

Putting your Panama property purchase in your own name is pretty straightforward. However, before you know whether to create a Panama corporation or foundation, you need to understand them better.

Post-Coronavirus

Lawyers are fully able to do the work to create corporations and foundations, even during quarentine.

Corporations vs Foundations

When choosing between holding your real estate in a corporation or foundation, your decision will depend upon how you will use the property.

If the property will generate income, it may be best to set up a corporation for tax purposes (except if you are an American, see below).

If you are going to live on the property, and will not be renting it out, you might consider a private interest foundation that can serve to hold your property, and also act as your living will.

The main difference between a private foundation and a corporation is that a private foundation cannot conduct income-producing business. However, a foundation can own investments such as real estate, other companies, stocks, bonds, etc.

Also a Panama foundation is not the legal personification of a person or group of persons. There are no particular owners within a Panamanian foundation. That is, the assets of a private interest foundation in Panama represent a separate legal identity from the personal assets of its Founder, Protector, Council Members or Beneficiaries. Typically, a foundation has a specific mission that benefits a group of individuals.

5 Reasons - Corporation/Foundation

There are 5 main reasons to have a corporation or foundation hold your property.

1. Estate Planning

First the good news: there is no estate tax in Panama. The bad news is that you cannot avoid probate if a property is held under a person(s) name(s). Probate in Panama is conducted in court. This process is usually long and costly, requiring that you hire an attorney to represent you.

In a nutshell, having a will won't save you from probate, unless your property is held in a corporation or a foundation.

No Right of Survivorship in Panama

Be aware that you cannot assume that the laws in Panama are similar to the laws of your home country. For instance, there is no 'rights of survivorship' in Panama.

That is, if a Panama property is registered under more than one person's name, it just means that each party owns a share of the total. When one owner dies, the property does not automatically pass to the surviving co-owner(s). In some instances, especially when the co-owners are not married, the deceased partner's share of the property may end up being passed on to his/her heirs.

This is true even if the person who co-owns the property with you has also named you as his heir in his will. This is true even if a Panamanian lawyer created the will in Panama.

However, all of this complexity disappears if the property is held in a corporation or foundation. In this case, it is a simple process to change the ownership.

In conclusion, the specter of probate is a good reason to use a corporation or foundation to buy property in Panama. As long as the corporation or foundation's shares are properly structured, you will avoid probate altogether.

2. Avoid title transfer & capital gains taxes - sorta

You will often be told that if you want to avoid Panama's transfer and capital gains tax when buying and selling land, you should use a corporation.

Yes, this is true; corporations don't pay a title transfer or capital taxes. However, they do pay an equivalent amount in share transfer taxes.

The seller pays both the title transfer and capital gains taxes. Between the 2 taxes, the seller pays a tax equivalent of 5% of the sales price.

Title Transfer Tax = 2% of sales price.

Capital Gains Tax = 3% of sales price or 10% of gain, whichever is lower

However, while a corporation is exempt from those taxes, it must pay an equivalent share transfer tax of 5%.

Share Transfer Tax = 5% of sales price.

Either way you effectively pay the same amount of tax. However, if you sell via a corporation you lose out on getting a refund if it turns out that your capital gain is less than 3% of the sales price.

3. Privacy Considerations

If privacy is your aim, you need to choose the right type of corporation and structure it appropriately.

To that end, there are 2 types of corporations in Panama, each with a different level of privacy.

a. **International Business Corporation (IBC).** An IBC requires at least 3 Directors and 1 or more shareholders who can enjoy participation privacy – for this reason, IBCs are also known as Anonymous Corporations. In an IBC the directors (president, secretary, and treasurer) are all listed in the Public Registry. These roles can be held by you, family members, partners, or by a nominee director service. If you use a nominee director service, you can have a higher level of privacy regarding your participation in the corporation. In addition, the names of the shareholders are kept private and are not publicly listed.

Keep in mind that you cannot maintain anonymity if you plan on getting a mortgage. When you apply for a mortgage, your loan documents will be publicly accessible. Plus the bank will require you to show up at the bank in person before they will approve your loan.

b. **Limited Liability Corporations (LLC).** Alternatively, you could choose to form an LLC. LLCs do not offer the same level of privacy as an IBC. If someone searches for a specific LLC in

Public Registry records, they will easily discover the names of the managers and partners of that LLC. An LLC requires a minimum of 2 Managers and 2 or more Partners. You are not required to have an equal partners, one partner could have only a 1% share. The names of all the managers and partners must be publicly disclosed in all registration documents. The object here is to provide more transparency. Such transparency is typically a requirement of a partner's country of origin, rather than a requirement of Panama.

IBCs and LLCs share similarities in that both are legal entities and they both limit a member's responsibility to his participation as a shareholder or partner.

Highest Level of Privacy

If maximum privacy or anonymity is your goal, you should first create a foundation and then an IBC corporation. The key is to have the private foundation named onto the board of your IBC corporation, so you are not named specifically as a board member. That structure will give you maximum anonymity.

4. Friendly Nations Visa Application

Another benefit of forming a corporation is that you can use your Panama corporation to establish residency under the Friendly Nations program. Creating a corporation is a fast and easy way to help qualify for the popular Friendly Nation visa.

After you receive your permanent residency status, you can terminate the Panama corporation. Maintaining your corporation means that you have to pay annual fees. If you are a US citizen you will also be required to report on the existence of your corporation as part of your tax return, even if your corporation holds zero assets.

5. Lawsuits

Another important advantage to holding your assets under a corporate structure has to do with lawsuits. In the case of someone who attempts to sue you, they would not be able to go after your property since you do not technically own it. Instead it is in the name of a Panamanian corporation or a private interest foundation.

Costs of Creating a Corporation

Of course, there are negative considerations when deciding to create a corporation. I list 4 of them below, including why Americans, in particular, should think carefully before creating a corporation.

Financial Costs

You must pay a lawyer to create a corporation or a foundation. After that, you need to pay an annual fee to keep the corporation or foundation active.

The typical cost for creating a corporation is from $1000 to $1500. The government then charges an annual fee of $300 for its right of existence. Additionally, the resident agent might charge his own fee to represent the corporation.

Note: if you feel your attorney is charging too much for this service, you could find an attorney with a more reasonable fee. It is a simple process to change your registered agent. You do not need to feel stuck with a lawyer as your registered agent just because you originally hired him or her to create the corporation.

Paperwork in Panama

Over time Panama corporations have grown more expensive and the paperwork associated with owning one has become more demanding.

In recent years, all Panamanian corporations and foundations, even those with no activity, are required to file annual financial statements with their registered agents. The goal of this new requirement is to increase transparency, something that has increased in importance in the aftermath of the Panama Papers.

Potential Paperwork - Esp for US Citizens

As you have probably heard, the IRS is very aggressive about collecting taxes from US citizens with overseas investments and income. Americans (US citizens and legal residents) that file taxes in the US are almost invariably required to file a form 5471 with the IRS. This is required if they are officers, directors, or shareholders in Panama corporations (or in certain corporations in other foreign countries as well). This is required even if the corporation has a net value of zero dollars.

Regardless of your citizenship, you should ask a tax specialist in your home country what reporting and tax requirements apply to owning a corporation in Panama.

Income Generating Property & Corporations - esp. for US Citizens

If you own real estate that generates passive income (e.g., a rental property) and is registered under a Panama corporation, you could be in for a big tax headache as a US citizen or legal resident. This is true even if it is not passive income, for instance if you run a business that is held by your corporation.

However if it happens, if you earn money with a Corporation in Panama, you will be required to file even more forms with the IRS. Keep in mind, all US citizens have to declare as income on all money earned in a foreign country.

Very few Panama attorneys fully understand the tax issues this may cause Americans. And frankly, some don't care much. They are more interested in the money they make selling you a Panamanian corporation than whether it is the best vehicle for you to hold income-generating property.

So keep all this in mind when your lawyer insists that you need to have a corporation. Remember, you do not need to hold your Panama property in a Panama corporation. And, I repeat, if you are an American, you may not want to hold income-generating Panama property in a Panama corporation.

Talk with your lawyer or tax accountant about other options. Perhaps an offshore corporation in another country, or some other solution, would give you the protection of a corporation, without the tax and reporting requirements.

Closing Your Corporation

Perhaps reading this information has prompted you to want to close your Panama corporation. The simplest way to close a corporation is to stop paying its annual registration fees. Eventually the government will drop the corporation from its records. You can check the status of your corporation by using this link: registro-publico.gob.pa/.

If you follow the guidelines established for closure by the Law 32 of Public Limited Companies, it will still take more than 3 years to close the corporation. What follows is a summary of those guidelines. First, the board of directors of the corporation needs to vote on a dissolution agreement. If they vote in favor, then the shareholders need to vote on it. If they vote 'yea', then a certified copy of the agreement and the addresses of the directors and officers must be published in a local paper. After all that, the corporation is considered dissolved, but not closed. (Note: A corporation cannot be dissolved until all outstanding debts are made to the Ministry of Economy and Finance of Panama.) The government does not consider the corporation closed until 3 years after that notice is published in the newspaper. Not a fast method.

Given all that, the easiest way to close a corporation is to stop paying your annual corporation fees. Regardless of how you close it, you are not required to pay a lawyer to close your corporation.

Final Words

The final decision to hold your property in your own name, the name of a Panama corporation, some other offshore corporation, or a private interest foundation, will depend upon your individual circumstances. A style that is right for one expat in Panama may not be beneficial to another.

I hope this chapter has provided you with enough information on this topic so you can make the best use of the advice of your lawyer and/or tax accountants.

Chapter 7

Benefits & Development Costs of Lots

»» ———————————— ««

Benefits & Development Costs of Buying A Lot

When exploring Panama real estate, one of the choices you will make is whether to buy land that already has a house built on it, or to buy land on which to build your house.

You will also discover there are many more building lots (i.e., land without a house) for sale than there are homes for sale in Panama.

This chapter covers the benefits of buying a building lot. More importantly, it explores the development costs you may encounter when buying a building lot.

A good understanding of development costs, as well as how those costs can vary, will help you determine if a specific building lot is a good buy or not.

Why Buy A Building Lot?

1. **Undeveloped lots are some of the most available and affordable types of property you can buy in Panama.** This means you are more likely to find a lot in the location you want at a price you can afford.

2. **Vacant lots cost less.** Somewhat surprisingly, if a lot has a building on it, even one that looks like it should be torn down, will be priced higher than a similar lot with no structure. Check it out for yourself. There must be some psychological reason for this.

3. **Investing in an undeveloped lot = very low overhead costs.** Typically, you just need to keep the lot fenced and the grass cut. Beyond that, very little maintenance is required.

4. **You get complete freedom to build & landscape the way you want and on your own timetable.** For instance, you get to decide:

   o The sweet spot for your home on the lot. Select the perfect place to capture your favorite views and to allow space for any outbuildings, fruit trees, etc.

   o The design of your home. You won't be modifying someone else's design. You can start with your own vision.

   o Locations for your garden & outbuildings. If you have never gardened before, this is the place to get started. To cultivate many species, you simply get a cutting, stick it in the ground, and water. If you plant in the rainy season, you can skip the watering part. The term tropical paradise fits gardening perfectly here.

More Remote = More Development Costs

Development costs include all the expenses necessary to prepare the lot to start building your new home. In Panama, you might decide to buy a lot in the middle of a jungle, with no infrastructure within miles — not even with road access. Or you might buy a beachfront lot, or a lot in a subdivision, that includes all services (i.e., water, electricity, sewer, garbage pickup, cable, even bottled water delivery and lawn service) you need in place, ready and waiting for you to build your home.

A lot that already has utilities as well as road access will have low development costs. On the other hand, a remote jungle lot would have sky-high development costs.

Calculate the True Cost of a Building Lot

Before you jump to the conclusion that an undeveloped lot is a screaming deal, you must factor in the development costs. That is, how much will it really cost to get the property into "ready to build" condition?

True Cost = Sales Price + 4 Cost Factors (described below)

You should calculate the true cost of a lot before you decide to buy. This is the case even if you don't develop it, but simply wait to sell it for a profit once property prices in the area rise. This is because your eventual buyer will be factoring in those development costs when deciding whether to buy the property from you. Therefore, you need to make sure you are buying a lot that will be attractive, and affordable, to any future buyers.

4 Development Cost Factors

- Access road and/or driveway
- Creating a flat and level building site
- Utilities (water, electric, septic/sewage)
- Distance from suppliers, builders, and labor

Road Cost Factors

The cost of road access (or driveway) will depend upon the lot's:

- Distance from access road
- Distance from contractors who can create an access road for a reasonable cost

- Topography-related drainage and erosion issues

If you fall in love with a lot that is far from an access road, it will obviously cost significantly more to develop than if your lot is near, or on, an already established access road.

If the property is on a steep slope, its location will open up a whole new realm of costs. Not only will your new access road cost a lot more, and take more time to create, but you will also have to deal with on-going erosion and drainage issues. Remember, 90% of the soil in Panama is silty/sandy in nature; only land near historic volcanic flows or river beds is rocky, so keeping soil from washing away is a big consideration. After all the work of creating a new road, you want to be sure that it will be usable for years to come, and not be transformed into a muddy disaster by the next big rain.

To keep road construction costs down, you should:

- Do the majority of the road work during the dry season, not the wet season.

Plus pick a lot that is:

- Near an access road. Ideally, a lot which already has a good road leading right to it
- Not in a hilly area or on a steep slope
- Near suppliers, contractors, and laborers

Your home construction project will cost more and take longer if your lot is located miles from the hardware store, backhoe operators, etc. Not only will you have to cover transportation costs, but also sometimes it is hard to find someone willing to schlep all the way out to your site when they have plenty of work right in town. This issue is more prevalent in Panama than it would be in North America. Panamanians are generally more concerned with lifestyle than profit. If the job isn't convenient, Panamanians are unlikely to do it - at any price.

The Building Site

Now that you can access the lot, you need to get it ready for building construction. The 2 most critical factors are:

- A flat and level place to build the house

- Providing all utilities to the site (electricity, water, and sewer or septic tank)

Flat and Level

Ideally, your site is already level. Or perhaps you simply need to remove some trees (just make sure to get a permit to do that) or you may only need a moderate amount of fill in order to grade the site.

If you are building on a slope, this will be more complicated. You may need a major earth re-grading project, including retaining walls and/or drainage system.

Make sure you get a good idea of the cost to achieve a buildable site. Otherwise your development costs may come as a big shock. To get a clear idea of the full cost, you also need to factor in the time required not just the money you will spend.

The less you have to do to make the site buildable, the better. A flat, level lot with good access can save you time, money, and headaches. There are plenty of these types of lots for sale.

Google Earth – A Real Estate Tool

You can discover if a lot is topographically challenged right from the comfort of your computer at home by using Google Earth. Furthermore, it will give you a feel for a property even before you visit it.

Google Earth is free and can be used with both Apple and PC computers. To use it, you will need to download the software. Then you can search for your property by entering its address or GPS coordinates.

If you don't know a lot's GPS coordinates or its address, you can ask the seller or realtor for them. Also, some property listings include a property's GPS coordinates. Another option to get the coordinates is to use another Google service: Google Maps. It is only a Google search away. However, that will only be effective if you can locate the lot by sight while using Google Maps.

Now comes the fun part. Once you have entered the GPS coordinates, you can zoom in by using your mouse/cursor and the command and shift keys on your keyboard. (Note: use the control and shift keys for PCs) Using the same controls, you can tilt the earth so you can view your prospective lot in profile, or at any angle. This allows you to discover precisely where all the hills and valleys are on the lot and in the surrounding area.

Utilities

Now let's talk a bit about providing utilities to your building site. Obviously, the best situation is if the utilities are already at the site. If there is a developer, who is obligated to provide services, make the details, including the timeline for providing them are in the purchase contract.

If you will be responsible for providing the utilities on your site, make sure to ask the availability of needed utilities, the process and typical timeline for getting the utilities to your site. For instance, is the site within the water district, or do you need a well, is there a sewage system or do you need to dig a septic system?

Electricity

Generally, electricity is available on most of the main roadways and neighborhood streets in Panama.

Remote Areas

If you are buying a remote property, you will be responsible for bringing in electrical power from the nearest road, where you will access it via overhead power lines. You will need to install your own power poles, or underground conduit, to deliver this power. And of course, you will need a licensed electrician to obtain an electrical permit, even if you plan to do your own electrical work.

Alternatively, you might decide to be completely off-grid. Just be sure to factor in the full cost of setting up and maintaining your own electrical power plant. Of course, if your lot is extremely remote, you will have no choice but to go off-grid.

Developed Areas

Panama is not a third world country in terms of its overall infrastructure. Developed areas generally have good access to power lines via the local electrical utility provider. This makes electrical installation simple.

What you need to do is:

- Obtain a permit at the local electricity office. (A licensed electrician must apply for the permit, even if you will do the work yourself.)

- Build an electrical meter mount. This is a narrow section of concrete block wall (24-36" wide), at your front property line, with a roof overhead to protect the electrical meter from rain.

- The electric company will hook up your meter to the overhead electrical lines.

Note: Once you start to build your house, you can connect the meter to the house in 2 possible ways. 1) You can run an overhead line from your electrical, which enters through the roof of your home or 2) You can dig a trench and install an underground conduit, with your supply cables running inside. These cables connect the breaker panel to the electrical meter at the property line. From the breaker panel, you can do your own rough in wiring. Or you can hire an electrician to do the installation.

Water

You must consider how you will get water to your lot and future house.

In Remote Areas

Before you buy a property in a remote area, make sure you know how you will provide water to the site. It is likely that you are going to have to dig a well. If you choose to dig a well, check with a civil engineer to verify that there are other wells in your area and how much water these provide. Also find out how deep a well you will need to dig. Then calculate the cost of digging the well and delivering the well water to your future house. If you are told there is a well on site already, verify the existence of this well and then test the water for quality.

About Digging Wells

The good news about well digging in the rural areas and small towns is that it is inexpensive. In most cases, wells are dug by hand, using a shovel. In most areas, the soil is silty/sandy, and it has no aggregates. (Note: this type of soil is not the most stable building substrate.) However, you should investigate the "digability" of the soil on your potential purchase. Obviously the harder it is to dig a well, the more it will cost.

In short, a laborer or two digs your well, and you line it with concrete pipe sections. These concrete pipe sections are typically available in 3-foot lengths and in many diameters from 10" to 2 or 3 meters.

Please be aware, hand digging can be dangerous for the laborer especially if the well is deep. You should check with the municipal engineer to find out the details for doing this safely, and if the person doing the work is covered by insurance. This work can be made safer by having the hole supported, or "cribbed" during the excavation. A fatal accident occurred in our town of Puerto Armuelles when a laborer was killed by concrete debris that struck him on the head while he was working in an uncribbed well.

The pipe sections used to line the well are very heavy. You will need to schedule a backhoe to have these installed. If you decide to use a backhoe for the entire well digging process, the result will be quite sloppy. Backhoes cut a very wide hole. All that dirt will need to be stored on site until it is back filled. The dirt excavated for the actual well will need to be stored or used permanently, on site, or hauled away.

Of course, you may decide to hire a well drilling company to do the work. These are usually located in more urban areas, but will likely travel to your site. For instance, there are companies in David that are happy to travel an hour or so to Puerto Armuelles to drill a well. You can search on the Internet for drilling companies near your property. Obviously, using a well-drilling company is the most expensive option.

Developed Areas

Almost all developed locations in Panama have access to a municipal water supply.

Connecting to Municipal Water Supply

To gain access to the municipal water supply, you simply cut a connecting hub, or collar, into the ABS water line that runs alongside the street nearest your lot. You can buy a connection collar at most local building supply stores. In our town of Puerto Armuelles, this ABS pipe is likely to be 3″ in diameter. I imagine it is the same for most other areas, other than Panama City where it is likely to be much larger.

You will need a permit both for the water supply line hook up and for any necessary street cut for the new pipe. You will only need a street cut permit if the city water line happens to be located on the opposite side of the street from your property. This street cut is performed by MOP (Ministry of Public Works).

You can apply for your own permit. However, for the $20 that my plumber charges to do all the legwork of obtaining permits, we never get our own permits.

Sewer or Septic Tank

In addition, you must include the cost of taking care of sewage and grey water from your home. The way you take care of this depends upon where your lot is located.

Out of Town or Remote Areas

Sewer service is typically only available if you are located in or near a town, or along a main road. In some places, you will need a septic tank even if you are near a road or town. However, if you are not in town, or on a main road, you will most likely need to install a septic tank.

When you are doing a construction project that is likely to be visible, or is going to be inspected, you should get a permit for all major plumbing projects, including a septic tank. A licensed plumber must submit the permit application, even if this plumber is not the person who is going to do the work. Talk to your neighbors to learn more about how this septic tank permit & installation process is usually done in your area.

Installation of Septic Tanks

There are a variety of methods for installing a septic system. The very poorest Panamanians simply dig a deep hole, line it with old car tires stacked one on top of another, and run their PVC waste line into it (or set an outhouse on top).

Most locals, who can afford it, build 2 separate septic tanks out of concrete block.

The first tank, in line from the house, captures the solids and lets the liquid flow off the top toward a secondary tank. This 2nd tank is filled with large round drainage rock. (This rock is available from local rivers. Local truck operators can deliver it to your building site.)

This second tank provides a drainage field that leaches out into the surrounding soil, and hopefully, filters out all dangerous bacteria, before they can get into local streams, or into the ocean.

Instead of installing a concrete block septic tank, you can purchase black plastic (ABS) molded tanks from local building materials suppliers, or from suppliers in larger towns like David. Most suppliers also offer delivery services to easily accessible locations. However, due to the silty nature of much of Panama's soil, the PVC tanks do not get enough support and have been known to collapse from hydrostatic soil pressure during the rainy season.

In Town – Sewer Connection

If your lot is in town, or on a major road, you can hook up to the municipal sewer system. To connect to the municipal sewer pipe on your street, again, you must apply for a permit. Again, a licensed plumber must file this application, even if this plumber is not going to do the work.

The connection is a simple matter of cutting in a connecting hub to the municipal sewer line, usually 6" PVC pipe. Generally, homeowners connect their own 4" PVC pipe to this 6" PVC pipe. It is a simple procedure. Pipes are not buried very deeply; generally, not over 3 or 4 feet deep. If your soil is silty/sandy, this kind of work can usually be done with a couple of laborers using hand shovels in half a day.

The entire connection process, including plumbing and backfill, shouldn't take more than a day once you have your permit.

Factor in Utility Costs

Before buying a lot, you should estimate the cost of permits, materials, and labor to get utilities to your building site.

Obviously, if all your utilities are already delivered to your lot, you will be saving yourself money and headaches. If your lot is in a remote area, your "get your site ready" development costs will be a significant part of the final cost of your lot. Don't forget to factor in the time it will take to get the infrastructure into place.

Is the Lot A Good Buy?

Is the lot worth the price? You first need to know the true cost of the lot.

True price = Sales Price + 4 Development Cost Factors

Calculating the true price allows you to compare seemingly diverse properties. For example, knowing the true cost of properties allows you to know which of these similarly sized and similarly located lots is a better buy:

- Lot for $10K - raw land with no road or utilities
- Lot for $30K - ready to build
- Lot for $80K with an existing, finished house

Final Words

Hopefully, you are starting to have a better understanding of the true cost of a property. As I explained, depending upon the location of a lot, preparing a lot for construction can vary dramatically.

It is something you should consider before buying a property.

Chapter 8

Financing Your Purchase

»———————————«

Property Finance

In addition to deciding where your new home will be, you'll need to figure out how you are going to pay for it.

Almost all properties purchased in North America are financed. That is not the case in Panama. Well, at least not for properties purchased by foreigners.

Most Purchases Not Financed

Most purchases by foreigners in Panama are made without financing.

Cash Payments

In Panama, most property is paid for with cash. Of course, this isn't actually a cold hard cash payment. Typically this payment is made using a cashier's check or a wire transfer from your bank account.

It is not recommended that you pay for a property with a suitcase full of cash, even if you have the cash on hand. It is always a good idea to have a paper trail of all payments you make on a property.

Post-Coronavirus

During the calendar year 2020, Americans have an improved financing source thanks to the Coronavirus Relief bill, known as the CARES Act (March 27, 2020).

The CARES Act allows people to withdraw up to $100,000 from their retirement savings (e.g., 401(k)s, 403(b)s, 457s, and Traditional IRAs) without the usual early withdrawal penalty of 10%. Plus, if you repay the withdrawal amount within 3 years, you don't need to pay taxes on it. Furthermore, if you don't repay the withdrawal amount, then you can pay the taxes on it over 3 years.

In addition, from April to September 2020, the CARES Act also doubles the loan amount people can take from their 401(k) plans. This means, you can get a loan of up to $100,000 or 100% of your 401(k) account balance, whichever is lower. (Note, you cannot take a loan from IRAs.)

These new CARES Act rules apply to Americans who are suffering from COVID-19, including those who have lost a job because of the pandemic or who have a spouse with the virus.

Overall, when considering any of the usual payment or financing options (listed below), if they can be done electronically they will generally be unaffected by the coronavirus quarentine and related restrictions. For instance, most, if not all, seller financing will not be impacted by the total quarentine.

If you are in Panama, depending upon your bank and location, you may still be able to apply for local bank financing. However, given the quarentine restrictions, you may have to complete the application over a longer timeframe.

Most types of financing are likely to still be available, although the process may take longer.

Financing Options

There are two main options for financing property in Panama.

- Seller financing
- Local bank mortgage

I review these, and some less commonly used financing options, below:

Seller Financing

Some sellers (like us) offer to finance your purchase of their property. This way you can avoid dealing with a bank or mortgage company. It can be very time consuming for a foreigner to get a bank mortgage in Panama.

Seller financing is a good option for buyers who want to buy a home in Panama but need to sell their current home to pay for it. In that case, a buyer may want to negotiate terms that include a small downpayment and monthly payments until their house back home sells (say 3 years), and then a balloon payment at the end of the 3-year term. You can have your lawyer or agent help you with this.

This type of seller financing allows you to secure the property of your dreams and allows you time to complete the sale of your house "back home". If the original home sells earlier than expected, then you get to pay off the balance early. Be sure your contract has no penalty for early payoff.

For buyers, who have monthly income and some cash-on hand, but not enough to pay for the property in full, they may ask to structure the financing to make a larger down payment of, say 30 to 40%, then pay the balance in monthly payments over 5 years or so.

Owner financing is a great option for buyers who know they want to purchase property in Panama but cannot pay for it fully upfront.

Local Bank Mortgages

It is not an easy process to get a mortgage through a Panamanian bank. It is tedious. And it can take a long time, especially if you are a US citizen.

If you plan to apply for a mortgage, allow for a good long wait before it is finalized and approved. Occasionally loans are approved quickly; although, this isn't likely. However, it will be a wonderful gift if it does happen fast.

The amount of documentation that is required will leave you flabbergasted. God forbid you forget to include a document or detail when you submit your application. Your omission can bring the whole mortgage application process to a crawl.

Big Development Exception

Purchases in large developments may have an easier time getting financing. This is especially true for large developments, especially the type that sell property in the pre-construction phase. This is because the developer is likely to already have a good relationship with a local bank.

In those situations, your loan can be granted in a matter of days.

Residency Not Required - Age Is A Factor

You do not have to be a resident to get a mortgage.

However, you do need to be less than 75 years of age (see below for more).

Top Factors to Qualify for A Loan

- Your ability to pay
- The loan to value ratio

In North America, qualifying for a loan is all about your credit history. However in Panama, the banks focus more on your ability to pay and the property's loan to value ratio.

Lots of Documentation Required

Because of this dual-focus, Panamanian banks require massive amounts of documentation.

Documents that:

- Verify your income
- Determine the value of the property you are buying

Property Eligible for A Bank Mortgage

Panama banks will only give loans on land that is:

- Titled
- Has had some improvements (i.e., such as a house, building, etc. with value)
- In an urban or developing area

Terms and Requirements

The following are typical mortgage terms and requirements for foreigners:

- The loan term must end by the time you are 75 years old. So, if you are 65, you can only get a 10-

year loan, but if you are 55, you can get a 20-year loan.

- 25 years is usually the maximum term of a loan, regardless of your age.

- Up to 75% of purchase price is the maximum financing you can obtain. Typical financing is for 60 - 70% of the purchase price.

- Purchase price cannot be more than the appraised value.

- Life insurance policy is required, with the bank listed as the beneficiary. This ensures that if you die before age 75, the policy will pay off the mortgage. Panama banks don't want your property, they just want your money: dead or alive. You are required to buy such a policy regardless of your age.

- Fire insurance is required and must cover 80-100% of the amount of the loan.

- You must physically appear at the bank to complete the loan application.

Required Documents

I advise you to ask multiple times about what documents are needed for your loan application. It is not unusual to submit your documents to the bank only to learn that they forgot to mention one or two other documents that you need to supply.

If you think you will be applying for a loan, you should bring some of these documents with you to Panama. Others you can gather in Panama. Most banks require them. Of course, every bank has slightly different requirements.

Some documents you may need or your loan application:

- Photocopy of entire passport (all pages and stamps)
- Photocopy of one additional photo ID (i.e., Driver's License)
- Utility bill showing your name and physical address
- Personal education and work resume
- Credit report from home country
- Proof of any down payment made
- 2 reference letters from your financial institutions

- Reference letter from another source (commercial, professional, or personal)

- Last 2 years of tax returns

- Asset verification (Bank statements for the last 12 to 24 months, retirement accounts, equity in your home, etc.)

- Letter explaining your income sources & reason for the purchase (e.g., primary residence, second home, rental, business)

- Appraisal of the property by a licensed appraiser

- Signed and notarized purchase contract

- Title deed of the property

- Completed and signed mortgage application

Banks typically require all documents (such as your bank statements) from your home country to be "authenticated" either through the Panamanian consulate or by "Apostille". An apostille is a globally recognized type of a government certified authentication of public records, which is why getting your documents apostilled is a better way to go than authenticated.

Some banks require that you have a Panama bank account for at least 6 months before you can qualify for a mortgage.

If you are self-employed, you will need to submit additional documents:

- Information about your company (name, physical address, phone numbers, website URL)
- A letter in which you describe the history of the company and the type of business it conducts
- Last 2 years of financial statements, which have been audited by a certified accounting firm
- 2 reference letters from clients of your company
- 2 bank letters of reference for your company

Credit Committee Review

Once all the required documentation is in your Panamanian bank's hands, it is sent to the bank's credit committee.

This Committee has 14 days to analyze your loan application. Once approved, you, the buyer, can review the terms.

If you agree to the terms of the loan, then you sign and return it to the bank.

The bank then issues a promissory letter for the approved loan amount.

Mortgage Interest Rates

Interest rates in Panama generally correspond with those offered in the USA. However, the interest rate in Panama is not driven by the borrower's credit-score.

Mortgage interest rates can vary depending upon the factors below:

- Type of property (personal residence, commercial property, investment property, etc.)
- Age of construction (new construction, old construction)
- Term of the loan (short term, long term, etc.)
- Applicants' age and visa status. (Pensionado visa holders can qualify for special mortgage interest rate reductions)
- Additional collateral offered to the bank as a guarantee on the loan.

Note: if you have a pensionado visa, you may be eligible for a discounted interest rate. You should ask the bank about that possibility.

Panama Preferential Interest Rates for Home Mortgages

Panama has a law to help first time buyers, including foreigners, of new homes by subsidizing the mortgage interest rate. Obviously, this is also great news for big developers. If you are looking to buy new, titled property with a loan of $35 to 120k, you might want to find out more about this program.

Things to Watch Out For

Items to be aware of while reviewing your loan documents include:

- Late payment penalties. Some banks include as much as a 2% interest rate increase for a late payment. In Panama, there are no "grace periods" for late payments. You may want to negotiate for a grace period.

- A clause requiring the payments be made to a "specific bank branch". This means you may not be able to make automatic mortgage payments, which can be extremely inconvenient.

- Some Panamanian banks have mortgage contracts preventing any pre-payments or reduction of principal for the first five years. If your loan documents contain such clauses, negotiate with the bank to allow for pre-payments. (See tip below for why you want to do this)

- Every bank in Panama will require fixed monthly mortgage payments. There are no adjustable interest rates in Panama. Each payment includes from 85% to 90% interest while the remainder goes toward the principal.

How to Pay Less Interest

Here are 2 tips to help you pay less interest over the term of your loan:

- Pay your mortgage bi-weekly instead of monthly. This will save you money and enable you to pay off your mortgage sooner. Bi-weekly mortgage payments involve making a half-month's payment every two weeks. That's 26 payments a year amounting to 13 monthly payments instead of 12.

The extra month's payment is applied directly to the principal. This can shave four years off a 15 year loan resulting in slashing your interest payments by 27%.

- Ask your lawyer or agent, especially if they have contacts at your bank, to negotiate with the bank to modify the loan document to be more favorable to you.

Because of the difficulty in obtaining a standard mortgage, many people, especially from the US, try to get around bank financing in Panama. This can include seller-financing (as discussed earlier in this chapter), developer financing, or borrowing in the US against your retirement.

Developer Financing

You might take out a loan from the developer of a property, rather than from a bank or mortgage company.

This is very common during the pre-construction or during-construction phase of development.

It usually consists of small down payments, small monthly payments, and then a balloon payment once construction of your property has been completed.

If a developer has a relationship with a bank, your loan can be pushed through within days, but only to buy that specific property sold by that developer.

Regional Bank Financing

In Central America there are international banks that provide mortgage financing for properties located in various Central American countries.

If you plan to invest in Panama as well as in another Central American country, you may want to develop a relationship with one of these international banks.

International Banks

International banks, such as Lloyds and TSB International, will finance properties in many countries. These larger banks will sometimes finance up to 70% of the value of the property.

It's possible that, though you had trouble getting financing for a specific type of property from one sector of the banking community, another sector will find your application more attractive.

List of Banks

Currently (in 2019), there are 67 banks (Regional, International & 2 State-owned) in Panama. Use the following link to see a list of Panama Banks maintained list of banks: www.panamabanks.info/list–of–banks–in–panama.

Self-Directed IRA

If you have an IRA at a traditional brokerage firm, you can roll it over into a self-directed IRA. Self-directed or self-managed IRAs give you complete control over selecting and directing where to invest your IRA. This can include real estate in the US or overseas.

However, this option is not for everyone. You need to be actively involved in managing your IRA and to learn the rules of the self-directed IRA. Also, depending upon how it is structured, this may generate taxable income.

You can learn more by reading the 2019 Guide To Self-Directed IRAs by US News & World Report or by asking your tax accountant.

Cash-Flow Properties

If you plan to make your first investment in Panama a cash-flow property, such as a rental, B&B or hotel, you can use the proceeds to buy or finance future properties.

CAP rates in Panama can be excellent. We know someone in Puerto Armuelles who pays rent of $500/month to an expat who had bought a rental house for $50,000. You do the math. Even without looking at the CAP rate, the investor is making 12% a year plus appreciation.

Final Words

If you want to finance your Panama property, seller financing is the fastest and easiest way to go. However, as noted above, you have other options as well.

Chapter 9

Before You Make an Offer

Ideally, you should have a lawyer lined up before you make any offer on a property. It is not necessary, but a good idea to have one to advise you. Plus all the paperwork will be in Spanish - Spanish legalese - so it is helpful to have a lawyer who is familiar with all the jargon, potential issues, and red-flags.

Before you make an offer, you should be very clear about what it is you are buying. I have outlined some things to ask and/or consider so you can ensure you are not unpleasantly surprised post-purchase.

About the Property

You need to make sure of what you are buying, not just the property boundaries, but other considerations as well.

First, is the property in line with your list of Where, What, When & How Much (see Chapter 1) Does the property offer your non-negotiable elements and amenities? For instance, is having a grocery store right around the corner important to you? or fast Internet? or space to build a shop? It is rare to find a property that meets 100% of your desires. However, you need to be happy with the trade-offs afforded by your selected property.

Are you clear about the property's boundaries, easements or other issues? Look at the survey, walk the property and make sure there are clear markers that indicate the boundaries of the property - typically done with corner markers and/or fences. Do the adjacent neighbors agree with the property lines? It is better to know about any property line disputes before you buy, instead of when you are installing a new fence post-purchase. Another thing to investigate is if there is public access or other easement through or near your property. Consider whether any such easement would negatively impact your living experience.

What's included in the sale? Anything that's considered a fixture is typically included when purchasing a house — think cabinets, faucets, and window blinds. However, there could be items that you think are included with the home but actually aren't. In the case of doubts – ask for a written list as an addendum to the contract. Keep in mind, washers & dryers, air conditioners and more are not usually included when purchasing from Panamanians.

What are monthly utility costs? This is particularly important in Panama – different areas of towns have different rates. The government subsidizes the costs in some areas, but not in others. You can't get away from paying utilities, but you should know what your monthly budget for these will be. Make sure to get an average cost — not the lowest monthly bill — and ask when peak months are. Typically, utility costs are very low. The exception is electricity if you use air-conditioning. In Panama, the price per kilowatt goes up dramatically the more electricity you use. So houses that run AC all day and night will pay much more for electricity.

Where does the water run-off go? Panama is a tropical country – it can have its-coming-down-in-buckets rainstorms. If you are buying a house, check out the gutters. Where do they empty? Is flooding an issue? Where does rainwater arrive into or out of your property?

Is there an issue or damage from termites, carpenter ants, or other pests? If you are buying a wooden house, this can be a particular issue.

What is the zoning on the property? Generally, most locations only have setback and height restrictions, but some areas have zoning that restricts use or density. As you could guess, Panama City has the most intensive use of zoning. You should make sure the zoning, if it exists, allows you to build the structure you want to build on it.

Neighbors & Neighborhood

You're not just buying a house; you're buying a neighborhood - and neighbors. You should find out more about both before making an offer.

If you see a neighbor, ask how they like living there. Specifically, ask questions, such as:

- Ask about any noise, odor, or traffic issues.

- What are the neighbors like - noisy or quiet?

- Is the neighborhood pet-friendly – is it safe to take your dog for a walk, or for it to wander off your property?

- Are there social venues or activities you can join to meet your neighbors and get more involved in the community?

About the Internet. You will find that some areas of Panama have high-speed fiber optics, while others max out at somewhere between 30-600 mbps. Another consideration is saturation. Some neighborhoods are saturated out with a specific provider. You may have been told that Cable Onda, for example, is a great Internet provider. You may also notice that many of your neighbors have Cable Onda. But when you call to get that service, Cable Onda tells you that they are unable to add new customers in your area.

What about future developments around your prospective new home? Will there be a nightclub, fish farm, or furniture-making workshop opening next door?

Is there a homeowners' association? What are the fees? What do they cover? It is important to know the rules of the HOA before making an offer. Also, find out what maintenance projects they've completed recently, what they plan on doing in the future, and whether people are generally happy with the HOA.

Costs to consider

As with buying property anywhere, investing in real estate in Panama comes with various fees and other costs. As you decide what to offer for a property, it is important to be aware of these costs. This knowledge can help in your decision and in your negotiations. For instance, during negotiations you can sometimes get the seller to pay for some of these fees and costs.

Here are some of the costs you're likely to pay as part of your purchase process - and afterwards.

- Your lawyer's fees. You should have an agreement that clearly outlines the lawyer's fees and what those fees cover so you are not surprised.

- Various banking fees for wiring money and so on

- Survey fees, if you decide to get a new property survey

- Annual property taxes on the property. (Find out about any property tax exemptions too)

- Utility costs

- Upfront HOA fees, if you purchase in the pre-construction phase. As well as on-going HOA fees, costs, and rules.

- Closing costs (For ROP, you only pay the notary fees):
  - Notary fees for the closing, plus the stamp duty
  - Public registry fees for registration of the public deed
  - Fee to update the tax department records after the sale has been finalized

Typically, the seller is responsible for most of the closing costs: paying realtor commissions, sales tax, capital gains tax, and any outstanding property tax and utility bills. However, if you buy from poor Panamanians, they will expect you to cover all the fees and expenses of the sale.

Large New Development Questions

Large developments promise to provide various amenities and services. Since these promised amenities are reflected in the price you are paying, you should get information on these as well as other aspects of the development.

Be clear on what is included in the house or condo you are purchasing. Developers in Panama will often deliver their units with all the floors and plumbing fixtures installed. However, in most cases appliances, air conditioning systems, lighting or curtains will not be included in the price.

Is the developer holding back the best inventory? If they are selling in stages, be sure you don't want to wait for another stage to make a purchase. Sometimes the best, or most expensive properties aren't offered in the early phases of a development. So be sure to study all its phases, before purchasing.

Is there a restriction on resale of your home? For instance, some developments won't allow you to sell your property - with or without a house - until they have fully sold all phases of the development. So if you were thinking of flipping your lot once prices go up, that won't be allowed.

Are you required to build a house on your lot within a specific timeframe?

Are you allowed to build a house of your own design on your lot? Are there design guidelines you must follow? or must you build a particular house? Can you build the house yourself or only using their contractor?

Ask the developer questions directly. Find out the status of the development financing, how is it regulating the project construction timeline? Are they on schedule with construction and sales? When do they anticipate the development will be finished? What is the developer's definition of "Substantial Completion"?

It may be different from what you are familiar with in North America or Europe.

Gated Communities Questions

Some people enjoy the benefits of a gated community. However, these are sometimes offset by restrictions and limitations. Be clear about what those tradeoffs are before you make an offer.

Property values

One of the benefits of a gated community is that if it is well designed, built, and maintained, its properties value tends to increase over time. Therefore, you should find out if property values are increasing or decreasing. What about in the surrounding area? Remember, towns and cities tend to retain or improve in value much more than remote developments.

Neighbors

In some parts of Panama, living in a gated community means that you are surrounded by expats. However, this is not always the case. Some gated communities; especially older ones will have mostly Panamanian neighbors, as well as a smattering of foreigners. Some people prefer a diverse community, and others do not. Make sure you are buying into your preferred community demographics.

You should also ask around if there are any issues with particular residents. Perhaps a neighbor who loves to work with loud power tools at all hours of the night. Howeve, most Home Owner Associations (HOA) would have noise restrictions prohibiting loud late-night activities.

HOA considerations

Living in a gated community means everyone has to abide by the rules - including you. There are often many rules. Rules governing your visitors, renting your home, group gatherings, exterior paint color, pets, landscaping, fencing and more.

If you are going to want to rent out your home, find out if there are any rental restrictions. Some HOAs restrict rentals, particularly short-term rentals. If so, you need to know how the HOA defines short-term. For instance, are air bnb type rentals allowed? Are long-term rentals allowed? How is that defined - 6 to 12 months, more or less?

Before you purchase, you should get a copy of the HOA rules and review them. Make sure you are happy with all the rules before you buy into the community. Don't think you can easily modify the HOA rules after you are a member. Changing HOA rules is rarely an easy task.

HOA payments, covered services and admin

You should make sure you understand the extent of the HOA. Below, I mention some of the items you should explore.

Which services & amenities are included in the gated community fees?

Ask to see a breakdown of fees that you are expected to pay – how many gardeners and workers are on the payroll?

How can you pay the fee? monthly, yearly, online?

Is a reserve fund set aside for major repairs or purchases? How much is in it?

Does the community have the funds for fixing the swimming pool, storm damage clean-up, rebuilding the gazebo, or re-paving the roads next summer?

Are people generally happy with the HOA administration?

Find out if there is any owner dissatisfaction or unrest with the HOA board that has oversight of the administrator.

Find out the date of the last HOA fee increase.

Have there been any special assessments in recent years? Are any expected? What specifically were these special assessments for? When do they expect to increase the HOA fees again? Who sets these fees?

Be sure to observe how well common areas are maintained.

Walk around the neighborhood and have a quick look at the common areas. Check that the roads are in good repair. Ask to see the beach club or social areas and make sure that the pool is not moldy. Are the street signs legible? All of these small details should give you an idea of how things are in the long run. Have there been any recent changes in the maintenance company or personnel? Are there any noticeable changes in the quality of the maintenance work being done?

Is residents' yard maintenance included?

While you are out-of-town, who maintains your yard? You should not assume that this service is included in your HOA fee. It may not be. However, you can probably pay extra for this service.

What architectural standards and guidelines are included in the HOA rules?

Are there restrictions on painting and modifications to the exterior of my home?

Are solar panels permitted?

What are the security features of the gated community?

Are there cameras and/or security personnel? What is the gate protocol for visitors and workers? How will your guests and visitors feel when they arrive at the gate? What are the protocols for announcing to the gate that you are expecting visitors? How will they treat unexpected visitors? Courteously, you hope.

How Much To Offer

This is the big question: What constitutes a reasonable offer. It could be that the asking price is reasonable and so, you offer to pay that.

However, in most prices there is some wiggle room, and sometimes there is a ton of wiggle room. The question is, how much wiggle room does this property have?

Unreliable Comparable Sales Info

In the US, you would look at comparable sales and base your decision on that and other factors unique to the specific property you are interested in.

Getting information on properties sold recently in Panama is more difficult. In the USA, all sales are posted to the MLS. It provides the asking price as well as the sale price, plus a wealth of other information.

There is no comparable MLS system in Panama. This makes it very difficult to determine value. You should not rely on what the real estate salesperson or the seller tells you. Even if you know of a property that sold recently, you don't know if the price you are being quoted is true. Both the seller and buyer could be exaggerating the price.

If you talk to the seller, they could be exaggerating in the upward direction to make it seem like they are a clever investor. The buyer, could exaggerate the price in the downward direction to make it look they scored a bargain. Or they could be telling you straight up, but without a functioning MLS you have no way to verify that.

You cannot even always rely on a recent purchase contract for the sale price. Sometimes, for tax reasons, the price recorded in the sale contract is lower than the actual price paid. This is especially true if it was an all cash sale.

Reasonable Offer

Yes, gather sales information, ask your realtor, other realtors, and expats in the area. Look at the various costs and other factors you learned about while investigating the issues mentioned in this chapter.

Obviously, the more time you spend in an area, the better sense you will get about prices.

Take your time, do your research, and only then, make an offer.

May Not Get Your Best Price

Remember, not every seller has to accept your best offer. Sometimes, you are not going to persuade a buyer to lower their price despite all your logic, charm and good intentions. They may place an unreasonably high value on their property, perhaps due to sentimental attachment. Or they recognize that they are in a market that is getting hotter and hotter and are in no hurry to sell. Or perhaps your offer really is not reasonable for that particular property.

If you cannot get a property for the price you want, don't worry, there is always another wonderful property out there.

Chapter 10

Real Estate Related Taxes

》》 ———————— 《《

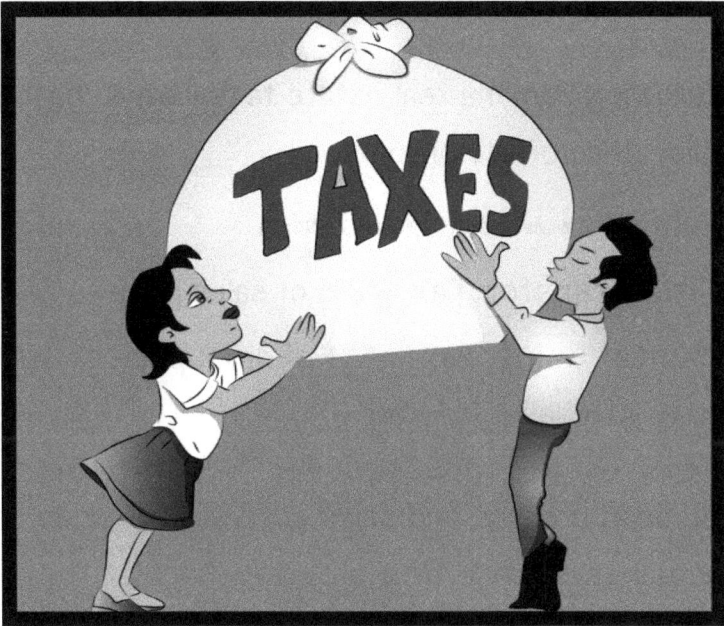

Panama real estate taxes are low.

- There is no inheritance tax
- Capital gains taxes are only 10% (max)

- And you may not have to pay any property tax – ever

In this chapter, I cover real estate-related taxes as follows: property, sales, transfer, capital gains, rental income, gift and inheritance taxes in Panama.

Panama Real Estate Transaction Taxes

The following Panama real estate taxes are all based on the sales price of the property.

- **Sales Tax** = 2% of sales price
- **Title Transfer Tax** = 2% of sales price
- **Capital Gains Tax** = 3% of sales price or 10% of gain, whichever is lower

Sometimes purchase and sales contract will understate the actual sales price of a property, so that the seller will only owe taxes on the lower, stated sales price.

This lower sales price decreases the tax bill. If someone asks you to do this, you must think carefully about whether it is in your interest or not.

Title Transfer Tax

The Title transfer tax is 2% of the updated registered value of the property or the sale price - whichever is higher. The updated value is the registered value, plus 5% per year of ownership.

Capital Gains Tax

The capital gains tax is a little complicated. The seller will initially be charged, and must pay, a tax of 3% of the sales price. After this payment, if 10% of the actual gain is less than 3% of the sales price, the seller can then apply to the government for a refund of the difference. However, receiving this refund can take a long time. Note: If the purchase contract is structured well, you will only pay capital gains tax on your improvements, not the full amount of the sale. Also, if you are selling furniture and other items as part of the sale, consider putting them in a separate contract so their value won't be subject to capital gains or transfer taxes.

Real Estate Taxes in Corporations

Homebuyers are sometimes advised to form a corporation to buy and sell property so they can then avoid paying title transfer and capital gains taxes. However, they will pay a 5% corporation share transfer tax, which is the same as the transfer and capital gains tax combined. **So taxwise, the cost is the same.** Also, they will not be eligible to receive a refund if their capital gain is less than 3% of the sales price.

In addition, there is an initial cost to create a corporation. Then there is an annual fee to maintain it in good standing. Of course, there are other reasons to form a corporation to buy property. However, if you are forming a corporation simply to avoid paying taxes, this is not the way to go.

ROP Exemption & Info

All real estate transaction taxes and property taxes are avoided if you are buying or selling ROP land.

However, if you plan to title your ROP land, then the sales price of your ROP property will be used as the tax basis to assess titling costs.

Property Tax

Panama recently passed a property tax reform bill. This represents a significant change to the tax system in Panama. The bill was passed to encourage owners to title their ROP properties.

As of January 1, 2019, there are higher exemptions from property taxes as follows:

- 1st $120,000 of value of your primary house is exempt
- 1st $30,000 of value of your 2nd home (or commercial or industrial properties) is exempt

Since most property in Panama is valued under $120,000, this means that most property in Panama will be exempt from property taxes.

In addition, the bill significantly reduced the property tax rate on primary residences. Prior to January 1, 2019, the max property tax rate was 2.1%, now the highest rate is 0.7%. Refer to the chart below for the newest property tax rates.

Current Panama Property Tax Rates

Effective as of January 1, 2019

Primary Residence	2nd Residence, Commercial & Industrial Properties
$0 – $120,000 = Exempt	$0 – $30,000 = Exempt
$120,001 – $700,000 = 0.5% tax	$30,001 – $250,000 = 0.6% tax
$700,000+ = 0.7% tax	$250,001 – $500,000 = 0.8% tax
	$500,000+ = 1.0% tax

Must Apply For Property Tax Exemptions

To qualify for an exemption on your primary residence in Panama, you need to officially declare it as your "Familiar Patrimony". You can only declare one property as your "Familiar Patrimony".

There is no deadline to apply for this exemption.

If your property still has an older tax exemption associated with it, you might want to wait to declare it as your "Familiar Patrimony" until after that older exemption expires. If you do it before the older exemption expires, you are effectively renouncing the older tax exemption on that property.

Apply for New Tax Exemption

If your property does not currently have an associated tax exemption, you should apply for the new tax exemption.

You can apply either online in the e-Tax 2.0 platform or in person at the Directorate General of Revenue offices. Here is the link to apply online: etax2.mef.gob.pa/.

For those homeowners who do not apply to register their property under one of the two property classifications mentioned above, then the current property tax rates will continue to apply.

Documents Required For Tax Exemption Application

Depending upon your situation, as you will read below, the document requirements vary.

Couples with or without children: Copy of IDs, Marriage certificate, Birth certificate of the children (when applicable), and Copy of the deed of purchase or certificate of incorporation for the property.

Individuals or Widows/ers: Copy of ID, Copy of the deed of purchase or certificate of incorporation for the property, and Certificate of death of the spouse (if applicable).

For Corporations: Copy of the ID for the legal representative of the company, Certificate of Incorporation, Copy of the deed of purchase or certificate of incorporation for the property, Certified letter from an accountant stating the members of the family are 100% owners of the entity, plus a sworn declaration by the shareholders declaring the property to be a family property (Familiar Patrimony).

For Foundations: Copy of the Deed of Incorporation, Certificate of Incorporation, and copy of the document that shows the beneficiaries of the Foundation.

If the Directorate General of Revenue does not contact you about your application within 3 months of submitting it, you can assume that your application was accepted. So in this case, no news is good news.

20-Year Property Tax Exemption Law: 2008-2018

Many people ask about Panama's famous 20-year tax exoneration law. Let me explain. Starting in 2008, Panama offered a 20-year tax exoneration for structures built before January 1, 2012. Then, in 2012, Panama added a tax exoneration for houses or condos built after January 1, 2012. However, it was not a 20-year exoneration. This tax exoneration varied from 5 to 15 years, depending upon property value. These older tax exonerations or exemptions will continue to apply until its term ends. However, these older exemptions, as of Jan 1, 2019, are not available to properties that are not already taking advantage of them.

While that law, which still applies to certain properties, was excellent, the new 2019 law is even better.

Once your current tax exemption has expired, you can still declare the property as "Familiar Patrimony" and then you will benefit from the new tax exemption.

Calculating Your Property Tax Bill

If you buy your primary home in Panama for under $120,000, you will not owe any property taxes since the first $120,000 is exempt from property taxes.

Panama's property tax is a graduated tax. The way this works is illustrated in the following example:

Let's say you bought a house for $200,000. After the $120,000 exemption, you would only owe property taxes on the remaining $80,000 of its value. This means, per the chart above, you would pay a 0.5% property tax rate on this $80,000. This results in you owing only $400 a year in property taxes on your $200,000 home, impressively low.

How To Lower Your Property Tax Even More

You can reduce your tax bill even more by paying the whole year's property tax in one payment. Panama grants you a 10% discount on your annual property taxes if you pay in one lump sum. Also by paying your property taxes on time, you can avoid paying late fees.

Don't Forget To Pay Property Tax

You will never get a bill for your taxes. It is up to you to remember to pay them – and on time!

Forgetting to pay your property tax in Panama is easy to do. As I said, property owners never receive a bill or reminder to pay the tax. No instructions are given on how to pay property taxes at the time of purchase. So unless you remind yourself, it is easy to forget to pay.

If you have a mortgage on your house the bank will collect the payments in an escrow account.

Post-Coronavirus

Due to the coronavirus, Panama has extended its property tax amnesty to June 30, 2020. It had expired in February.

You can use this amnesty deadline to your advantage in your proprety price neogiations. If a seller owes an outstanding property tax bill, he can save money by selling the property before June 30th. As I mentioned, the seller must always pay all outstanding taxes at the time of sale.

FYI: This extension does not forgive all fines and interest due on the late property tax payments. The extension offers an 85% forgiveness of fees and interest. If paid prior to July 1, an outstanding property tax payment will be for the property tax plus only 15% of any accured interest and penalities.

Property Tax Due Dates & Fines

Panama property taxes are due 3 times a year: April 30th, August 31st and December 31st. Payments after each due date have a 10% surcharge)

If you don't pay your property taxes, the government will garnish them when you sell your property, plus any interest and fees that are owed due to any late tax payments.

In the appendix, I have a section on how to pay your property taxes.

Rental Income Tax

If you rent out your property, you may need to pay tax on the income.

Rental income is taxed at the following progressive rates:

- 0% – rental income up to $11k/yr
- 15% – rental income 11k – $50k/yr
- 25% – rental income $50k – $200k/yr
- 30% – rental income over $200k/yr

Exemptions

If you own a hotel or condo-hotel in one of Panama's special "tourism zones," you may be exempt from income tax for 15 years.

Deductions

Panama allows the following deductions when calculating your rental income:

- Municipal and national taxes
- Maintenance and repairs
- Administrative expenses
- Depreciation of the property

I recommend you talk with your lawyer to find out if you will owe taxes on rental income.

Inheritance & Gift Tax

There is no inheritance tax in Panama. However, there is a gift (inter-vivos) tax on properties located in Panama.

The gift tax rate depends on the degree of relationship between the donor and the recipient. You should speak with your lawyer for the details. This tax does not apply to gifted property located outside of Panama.

USA, Panama Real Estate & Taxes

If you are a US citizen or resident, you can discover how to avoid double taxation, use loop-holes and more by reading US Taxes & Panama Real Estate in the Appendix.

Disclaimer: I am not a tax accountant. While I do research to make sure everything in this guide is accurate, you should consult a knowledgeable tax accountant when making your tax-related decisions.

Chapter 11

Translations, Contracts & Payment Methods

»» ———————— ««

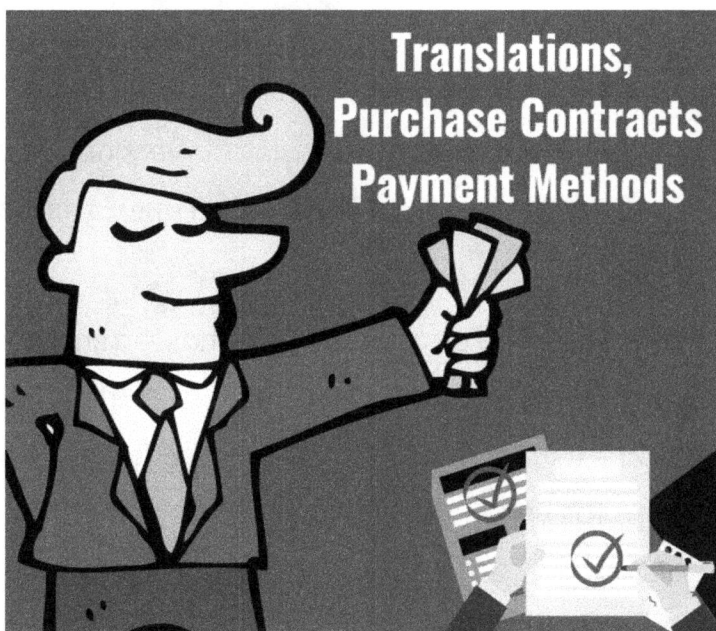

Before you buy Panama real estate, it is helpful to know about Panama's purchase and sale contracts, payment methods, and how to deal with all the paperwork being in Spanish.

Spanish & Translations

Unless you know Spanish well it is important that you obtain a good English (or whatever your native tongue is) translation of the contract. You want to have a clear understanding of what you are signing.

Be aware that when you go to sign the purchase agreement in front of a Public Notary, you will be asked if you understand Spanish. If you say that you don't, you will need to have a translated version of the documents - stamped by a Panama certified translator - in hand.

Thankfully, it is not difficult to get those translations, particularly if your native language is English. Your lawyer can usually provide the properly translated documents for you.

Whether To Hire A Lawyer

Which brings up the topic of lawyers. My husband and I have purchased many properties without the use of a lawyer. However, my husband is fluent in Spanish and we have had plenty of time to spend on and to learn the process. For most people that is not the case;

therefore, I recommend finding and using a good lawyer.

(For tips on finding a good lawyer, see chapter 5 about lawyers.)

Purchase Contract Options

Real estate purchases in Panama typically involve two contracts:

1. Promise to Buy (or Buy-Sell) Contract - which is optional

2. Purchase and Sale Contract

Both types of contracts are binding for both parties.

Although the Promise to Buy contract is optional, you may want one to ensure that the property is taken off the market while you conduct your due diligence and possibly obtain financing. Registering the promise document at the Public Registry is the best way to ensure the property won't be sold in the meantime. However, if you don't trust the seller not to sell while the property is under contract, you may want to think twice about dealing with that seller.

Promise to Buy Contract will include the following details:

- Price of property
- Deadline for Title Transfer
- Legal description of the property
- Any other stipulations and details that are important to the transaction
- Usually requires an earnest money deposit, which is typically around 10% of the purchase price
- Normally there is a penalty if either party backs out, except if there is a failure to meet a contingency or condition

Only enter into a Promise To Buy Contract if you are positive you want to go ahead with the transaction, subject to any contingencies.

Make sure all those contingencies are clearly described in the contract.

Purchase and Sale Contract

Purchase and Sale Contract will include all relevant items in the promise to buy/sell contract. In addition, it will include any financing terms, if seller-financed.

The Purchase and Sale Contract will be registered at the Public Registry and the final balance is paid to the seller, or in some cases, if an escrow agent is used, payment is made once the title is transferred to the buyers' name.

4 Ways To Pay

There are a number of ways to pay for property in Panama. I list 4 common methods below:

1. **You can pay in cash.** If you do so, make sure you pay the seller in front of the Notary. That way there is an official witness of your payment to the seller. This method is very common in Panama.

2. **Pay with a certified check or money order from your Panama bank.** You can wire money from your home country bank to your Panama bank. The wire transfer from a US bank is simple, since there's no currency exchange, and generally

takes around three days to be credited on the Panama side. A wire transfer from other countries is also relatively easy. You can then pay the seller, in the form of a certified check, once all obligations of the purchase contract have been met. Again, it is a good idea to present the check or money order in front of the Notary Public. If you don't have a bank in Panama, you can use option 3 below:

3. **Through a bank or escrow company in Panama**. You would wire transfer the property payment to the bank or escrow company. They would then issue an irrevocable letter of payment. In this letter, the bank or company irrevocably promises to pay the amount owed to the seller immediately upon the transfer of the title or completed conditions. The bank or escrow company will help ensure that everything is in order before they turn over the money to the seller. You would then authorize them to issue the funds, in the form of a certified check, to the seller.

4. **Have your lawyer make the payments**. You can transfer the money to your lawyer, and have him or her distribute the property payment(s). If

you feel confident in your lawyer, this is an excellent method since they are very familiar with the terms of the contract. However, some attorneys aren't willing to be involved in this step. If you want a 3rd party to make the payments, using a bank or private escrow company, or even a friend may be a good option.

Final Words

Overall the process of buying property is fairly simple and easy. The most likely issue you will encounter is delays in getting a final draft of the purchase contract done to the satisfaction of all parties.

Chapter 12

6 Steps to Buy Titled Property

»» ———————— ««

Congratulations! You found a wonderful titled property you want to buy. Let's assume that you have already considered all the issues about buying property that I raised in Chapter 9, Before You Make An Offer. In that case, it is likely a fabulous choice for you.

You will need to accomplish various tasks to fully vet and become the new, legal owner of a property: verify the title & ownership, ensure there is a survey of the property, perform other due diligence such as ensuring all utilities and property taxes are up to date, agree on the price and terms, sign a purchase contract (and prior to that, possibly a promise to buy contract and an earnest deposit as well), pay for the property, and get the title transferred into your (the buyer's) name.

You can accomplish all of these tasks in a 6 step process.

The 6 Steps

1. Negotiate the Price & Agreement

First and foremost, you and the seller need to agree on the price and details such as the time frame to perform due diligence. Your lawyer or agent can help you negotiate these terms.

When negotiating the price, make sure the seller includes all transaction costs so that there won't be any surprises regarding taxes, closing costs, etc.

A strong offer from you should probably include some sort of earnest money deposit on the property. Typically, you would provide earnest money in exchange for the seller taking the property off the market while you perform your due diligence.

You and the seller should be clear about what happens to the earnest money payment if you decide not to buy the property. Typically, if after investigation, the property characteristics are different from what the seller purported, you, as the buyer, would get the money returned. However, if you simply change your mind about buying it, not because of a significant issue with the property, the seller would keep the deposit.

Keep in mind, that if you are buying directly from a Panamanian, as opposed to an expat, you are less likely to get agreement on an earnest money refund. Although this is changing, even getting a return on merchandise at a store in Panama is difficult. It is just a concept that is not widely practiced in Panama. Plus if you are buying from a poor Panamanian, the money will most likely be spent by the time your due diligence is complete and there will be no refund.

Even if you decide not to take step 2, below, signing a promise to buy-sell contract, you should still take the prudent step of putting the details of ongoing conversations and negotiations between the seller and you in writing and, whenever possible, have both parties initial each item and sign each page. That way, when you have the final documents drawn up, there will be a clear record of any conversations that resulted in mutually agreed upon alterations, great or small, to the original contract guidelines.

2. Promise to Buy-Sell Contract

If you want, you can skip the promise to buy-sell contract and go immediately to the final purchase and sale agreement. It all depends upon how you and the seller have negotiated payment and terms. In Panama it is common to do both of these contracts. Find out more about the 2 contracts, in Chapter 12: Translations, Contracts and Payments.

At this point, if you are using a lawyer, he or she should write a first draft of whichever type of contract that you have opted to use. Panama has a very relaxed business culture, where the "Manana" attitude prevails.

For this reason, you should make sure your lawyer understands you want to have a translated version of the contract several days before going to the notary to sign. This will ensure there will be time to make any corrections or changes.

Keep in mind it can take days or even weeks to have a contract written, and translated into English (or whatever your native language is) by a Licensed Translator, depending on your location. (Note: Documents are not valid if the translator is not government certified and can stamp the documents with his/her Panamanian Translator's Stamp).

Do not allow your lawyer to wait until the last minute to draw up the contract. Remember, Panama has a very relaxed business culture, where the "Manana" attitude prevails. Without securing a clear understanding, it is quite common in Panama to arrive at the notary to sign a contract, only to discover that the lawyer charged with preparing the documents hasn't even begun writing it

If you find yourself being rushed through the notary's office, at the last minute and then handed a pen with which to "sign an important business document."

STOP! It isn't necessarily that anyone is trying to scam you. Most likely, it is just that the lawyer and/or property owner simply want to get paid quickly. However, you shouldn't give in to the pressure to sign now.

Make sure you have time to understand what you are signing, to ensure that it has all the terms you expected and no unexpected clauses added. <u>This is not a luxury</u>. This is a prudent strategy when making a large purchase, be it in Panama, or in North America. Protect yourself, by insisting that the documents be ready in advance. It is not your job to be rushed into signing a contract that is "hot off the press" just because your lawyer procrastinated until the last minute in preparing these documents.

A Promise to Buy-Sell Contract should include the following details:

- Price of the property
- Legal description of the property
- Any other stipulations and details that are important to the transaction.
- Deadline for Title Transfer

- Usually requires an earnest money deposit, which is typically around 10% of the purchase price
- Contingencies or conditions for which either party can legally, without penalty, back out of the contract

Normally there is a penalty if either party backs out, except if there is a failure to meet a contingency or condition. Make sure all those contingencies are clearly described in the contract.

Only enter into a Promise To Buy-Sell Contract if you are positive you want to go ahead with the transaction, subject to any contingencies.

If it has not already occurred, a small earnest money payment is made at this point. This payment will secure the property while due diligence is performed. It also allows you time to secure financing and create a corporation, if you are doing either as part of the purchase process.

To ensure that the property cannot be sold to any third party prior to closing, the promise contract should be registered at the Public Registry.

3. Due Diligence

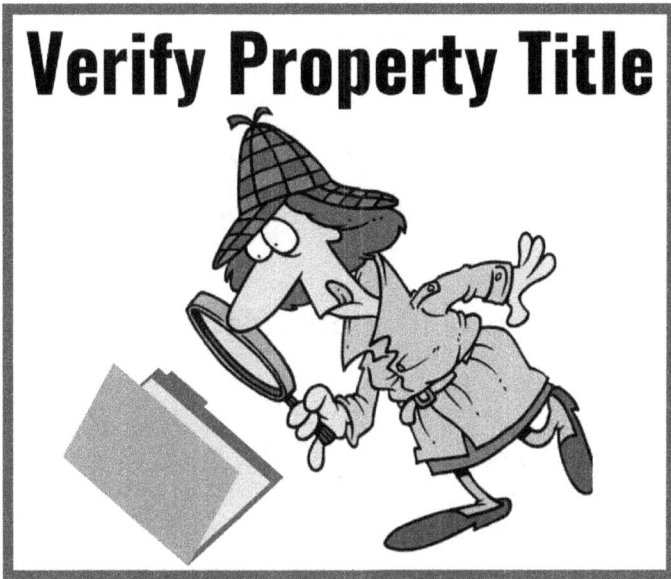
Verify Property Title

Most sellers are very transparent about the conditions of a property and its legal status here in Panama. However, there is always the possibility of a clueless or dishonest seller or realtor. As I mentioned in Chapter 5, there is no code of ethics for real estate agents in Panama. To protect yourself, you should consider hiring an experienced real estate attorney.

An experienced real estate attorney will be able to discover and defect or concern related to the property you want to acquire.

Due Diligence Tasks

You, or your lawyer, must do a complete due diligence on the property.

First, you must confirm that the property is really titled, and titled in the seller's name(s).

The seller should provide you with 2 documents:

- The title, also called the public deed or escritura
- The Ownership and Encumbrances Certificate (Certificado de Registracion) issued by the Public Registry (Registro Público).

It is possible that the seller does not have these documents. If they don't, ask for the assigned property number, which is often called the finca (ranch) number.

If the seller doesn't have these documents, I recommend an even more careful examination of the title to ensure the property you are buying is the same as the one you are researching.

Research Title, Liens, Easements & More

With the finca number you, or your lawyer, can search for the title at the Public Registry. The Public Registry now has a website that greatly assists in this search. Go to the Public Registry's website: registro-publico.gob.pa.

You should hire a competent Panama real estate lawyer to do a title investigation consisting of:

- Confirm that the property title at Public Registry is in fact in the name of the seller, and it is free and clear of encumbrances, liens, or other issues that could affect the free disposition or transfer of the title such as pending mortgages or court cases.

- Request an updated Certifiado de Registracion from the Public Registry.

- Review of cadastral survey map(s). In some cases, you may want a licensed surveyor to physically verify the property's map points, to avoid future boundary conflicts.

- Discover if there is money owed for utilities (water and sewage, power, telephone, etc.).

- Check to see if there are any easements, or other encumbrances to the property.

- Confirm that the property taxes are paid up-to-date (Remember: Titled Property is taxed every year).

- You should accompany your lawyer to conduct a thorough property inspection. If the property includes a house, or other structure, this step is especially important, since you may learn more about the condition of the building, and what your likely scope of work will be to complete any remodeling you have in mind.

Once the Public Registry issues a signed and stamped Certificado de Registracion, you will have verified the owners of the property, its location, and that it has no liens or other complications.

Is There A Property Survey?

An aspect of the due diligence that needs special attention is the property's boundaries. It is important that you are crystal clear on the boundaries of the property you are buying. You should walk the entire property and locate the survey markers. There should be one at each corner. We recommend that you ask the seller's permission to hire a laborer, or local contractor, to install concrete markers at each corner marked by the surveyor, if none are present.

If no survey has been done, I recommend that you hire an engineer and have a new survey done, using GPS coordinates, since this is the new legal standard. You may also want to get a survey done if the existing survey was completed in the 1940s, 50s and 60s, as the survey done then were generally not very accurate.

Check out Chapter 9: 9 Steps to Protect Your Real Estate Investment, for more details on what to include in your due diligence process.

4. Enter Into Purchase Agreement

Once both buyer and seller are ready to close the deal, the Final Purchase Agreement is signed before a local public notary.

A Purchase and Sale Agreement should include:

- Price of the property
- Legal description of the property
- Relevant payment information, if seller financing
- Deadline for Title Transfer
- Indemnification clause in the event of hidden defects of the property
- Usually requires an earnest money deposit, which is typically around 10% of the purchase price

- Contingencies or conditions for which either party can legally, without penalty, back out of the contract

The official sale contract might take a week or more to be ready because there are really no standard contracts in Panama.

Post-Coronavirus

At the start of Panama's coronavirus quarentine, it was not possible for the Public Registry to issue a new deed for a newly purchased titled property. This was because prior to issuing a new deed, the required tax forms had to be submitted and processed. Unfortunatley, initially, it was not possible to electronically submit those forms. Thankfully, in response to this need, the tax office has now created the ability to submit the required tax forms (106/107) via their online portal. This means the Public Registry can now issue a new deed in the new property owner's name, and complete the purchase process - even during Panama's total quarentine.

5. The Closing & Title Transfer

This is the exciting step, when you actually own the property!

Of course, the critical step for ownership is to fully pay for the property (otherwise known as closing on the property). Your purchase contract will describe whether you pay the seller in full (or final payment) at the Public Notary office or appoint an escrow agent (lawyer or banker) to pay the seller once the title transfer is recorded at the Public Registry Office or some other method.

Regardless of how you pay for the property, to transfer the title into your name the following documents need to be submitted to the Notary Public: the old title, previous land documents, and the new tax form.

The Notary will then type up the new title with the new owner's name, the seller's name, a description of the property, the location of the property, and any special terms that may apply. There is a minimal fee to do this.

Once this new title is written up and approved by the Notary's office, both the buyer and seller need to sign it.

In some cases, if the title is in a corporation's name and the seller agrees to sell the corporations' shares, then there is no transfer of title, only a transfer of shares of the corporation.

6. Register Your Purchase

You must sign the new deed (i.e., title transfer) and register it at the Public Registry. Your purchase is not fully final until you register it at the public registry.

After 10 days to a few weeks, you can go to the Public Registry to pick up your signed and stamped title to your property.

Congratulations! You are now the proud owner of a piece of land in one of the most popular destinations for expats and investors! Welcome, and enjoy all the natural beauty and wonder that Panama has to offer.

Chapter 13

How to Buy ROP Property

»» ———————————— ««

Congratulations on finding a fabulous ROP property! The process for buying ROP property is similar to buying tilted property. The most noticeable difference is that the due diligence process is more intensive for ROP property.

1. Negotiate the Price & Agreement

First and foremost, you and the seller need to agree on the price and terms such as a time frame to perform due diligence. Your lawyer or agent can help you negotiate these terms.

A monetary deposit of some amount is almost always needed to demonstrate that yours is a serious offer to buy the property. In exchange, the seller will take the property off the market for the agreed upon due diligence period.

The seller keeps this deposit if the buyer backs off for no reason. Likewise, the deposit is typically returned to the buyer if due diligence reveals a defect or concern about the property.

You should put your agreements about the earnest deposit, time frame for due diligence in writing (and initialed by both parties), even if you don't take the more formal step signing a promise to buy-sell contract. This written document is good to have so that both parties are clear on the terms and it will help resolve any future lapses in memory of those terms.

2. Promise to Buy-Sell Contract

If you want, you can skip the promise to buy-sell contract and go immediately to the final purchase and sale agreement. It all depends upon how you and the seller have negotiated payment and terms. In Panama it is common to do both of these contracts. Find out more about the 2 contracts, in Chapter 12: Translations, Contracts and Payments. At this point, if you will be using a lawyer, he or she should help create a Promise to Buy-Sell contract.

A Promise to Buy-Sell Contract should include the following details:

- Price of the property
- Legal description of the property
- Any other stipulations and details that are important to the transaction
- Usually requires an earnest money deposit
- Contingencies or conditions for which either party can legally, without penalty, back out of the contract

Only enter into a Promise To Buy-Sell Contract if you are positive you want to go ahead with the transaction, subject to any contingencies. Make sure all those contingencies are clearly described in the contract.

3. Due Diligence

You need to complete the same due diligence on ROP property as for tiled property. However because its ownership is not verified and registered at the Public Registry, you must investigate the property's ownership.

Verify its ownership history. Since most ROP properties are not registered with the State, you need to make sure that the person selling you the property really owns it.

ROP Records

ROP transactions are not recorded with Panama's Public Registry as is done with titled land. However, at times agricultural ROP land may be recorded with the Ministry of Agriculture Agrarian Reform offices. Also, some ROP beachfront, islands, and marine properties are recorded with the Directorate General of the Surveyor in the Ministry of Economy and Finance.

You can also sometimes find an ROP property's certification at the regional real property tax offices (Catastro), local Mayor's office, or local justices of the peace (Corregidora) or public notary (Notaria Publica) offices.

If the paperwork is not recorded in any of these government offices, (Catastro, Reforma Agraria, Mayor / Alcalde, Chief of Police / Corregidor, one of them can certify the Rights of Possession status.

However, that is not needed. The most critical ROP records you need are the original (emphasis on original, not copies) documents that illustrate the property's purchase and sale history. The current owner should possess these. You need to ask to see this paper trail so you (or your lawyer) can track the property's ownership history. A good lawyer can help you with obtaining these documents as well as to investigate the property's history per those documents.

If a seller does not have, or will not show you, these property documents, do not buy the property.

Post-Coronavirus

As I stated in Chapter 3, during Panama's total quarentine, a comprehensive ROP due diligence process will be more time-consuming to complete. Given social distancing and the very limited time people are allowed to leave their homes, it will be hard to contact neighbors in person. You may want to ask them for their cell phone numbers so you can ask them about the property and it ownership over the phone.

You may also want to consider a simplier, faster, and more secure option. That is, focus on property that has already been fully investigated and vetted. To ensure that the property has been fully vetted, ask the owner to digitally share the property's paper trail. They should be able to provide those documents.

If you are interested in Puerto Armuelles, you should check out our properties for sale using this shortlink: lynx2.co/sliceliprop. We have already fully vetted our properties.

Note: If you need a new survey done, during the total quarentine you cannot get it done. Surveryors are not considered essential workers.

Therefore, during Panama's total quarentine, surveyors cannot legally work. Hopefully, they will be able to start work again soon.

Due Diligence Tasks

Before you buy ROP property in Panama, do the following:

- A critical step is to review the paperwork trail showing the history of who has bought and sold the property over time. Make sure there is a clear succession of ownership, directly leading to the current owner(s).

- Make sure the seller has sole and full authority to sell the property. When conducting your review of the paperwork be aware if one of the property owners, as recorded in the most recent document, has died. This is because, in Panama, unless there is a will that states otherwise, each of that now deceased owner's children and spouse now have an ownership share of the property. It is a good idea to get a document signed by these potential "owners", whether it is a brother, wife, or child, to sign a document stating that they have no interest in or claim to the property. This will save you from someone appearing at the 13th hour saying he or she also has a stake in the property.

- Talk to the neighbors. Ask who owns the property. Make sure it is the seller. Ask about the history of the property and if there is or has been any conflict about who owns the property. Also ask about any easements. Does the property have an easement? If so, what kind and where is it located? Asking the neighbors about these issues may seem too simplistic, however, it is a pretty reliable tactic in Panama. In Panama, especially in small towns, there are no secrets.

After you verify ownership, you need to do the rest of the due diligence, as you would for a titled property:

- Make sure there is a survey. (In Spanish, a survey is called a plano.) If there is no survey or it is very old, get a new survey done. In some cases, you may want a licensed surveyor to physically verify the property's map points, to avoid future boundary conflicts. Put survey markers at each corner of the property. This will ensure that everyone agrees upon the property borders. If the owner and/or neighbors state that there is an easement, make sure it is shown on the survey.

- Find out if there are any bills owed at that address. In particular, electricity and water bills. Make sure the seller pays them before you buy. Or pay them yourself. It usually isn't much, but it is better to know about these bills before rather than after you buy.

Is the Property Occupied?

If yes, then do not buy it until 1 of 2 things happen:

1. It is vacant – with no one living in the house or on the property.

2. Sign a rental agreement with the current tenants. This ensures they cannot claim they own it simply because they are occupying it. It also allows you to evict the tenant once the rental term has expired. Make sure the contract is signed in front of a notary. You may also want to register the rental contract with the Ministry of Housing. If you do that, you can call on the Ministry to enforce the terms of the contract if needed.

Check out Chapter 15: 9 Steps to Protect Your Real Estate Investment for more details on what to include in your due diligence process.

4. Enter into Purchase Agreement

Once both buyer and seller are ready to close the deal, the Final Purchase Agreement is signed before a local public notary.

A Purchase and Sale Agreement should include:

- Price of the property
- Legal description of the property
- Relevant payment information, if seller financing
- Indemnification clause in the event of hidden defects of the property
- The official sale contract might take a week or more to be ready because there are really no standard contracts in Panama

5. Closing on Property

Pay for the property, either in full, or make your final payment on the property. At that point, the seller will provide you with all the original documents, which shows the ownership history of the property, as well as the original purchase and sale agreement you just fulfilled, and the property survey.

You also need to make sure the owner assists you in getting the property's electricity and water in your name.

If you desire, you can also start the process to title your property. I have a guide on my site on the titling process.

3 Things To Do After Buying ROP Property

Congratulations on your property purchase! Don't crack open the champagne yet.

You must make sure everyone knows you - and only you – now own the property.

Do These 3 Things ASAP

To make a public declaration of ownership you should do at least one of the following, ideally, all three. If you had to pick just one, the most important is to keep the grass cut.

1. Erect a fence along the property lines. Fence is already there? Then paint the fence.

2. Put up a sign stating, "Propiedad Privada, No traspaso" (that is, "Private Property, No Trespassing") with your name and contact information.

3. Have someone keep the grass cut. Make sure to obtain signed receipts from all workers you pay to cut the grass or do other maintenance on the property. Keep all these receipts.

Another way to assert ownership is to build a rancho or some sort of structure on the property.

These measures will ensure that everyone is aware that the property is owned and cared for by you. You don't have to be there yourself. The fact that you are hiring someone to cut the grass is enough.

Remember, one of the proofs of ROP land ownership is evidence that you are occupying the land. In Panama, maintaining the property is considered one way to prove you are "occupying" the land.

If there is ever a legal challenge, the court will ask for your proof of ownership. That is when you pull out your receipts of ongoing maintenance.

Did you buy a house?

If you won't be living in the house for a long period of time, you should consider doing 1 of 2 things:

1. Rent it for profit

2. Rent it in exchange for caretaking

Many people will recommend you get a caretaker for the property during your absence. (NOTE: In Spanish, a caretaker is called a cuidador or Guachimán. Guachimán is Spanglish word, pronounced, wah-chi-man) A cuidador is an employee who will sleep there (or in an outbuilding) at night and generally keep your property safe. However, having an employee comes with a host of other issues which if you can avoid, you should.

Rent for Profit

If it is a nice house that someone would eagerly move into and enjoy, rent it at market value.

Don't forget to get a signed and notarized rental agreement. You may also want to register the rental contract with the Ministry of Housing. If you do that, you can call on the Ministry to enforce the terms of the contract if needed.

Rent in exchange for Caretaking (Cuidador)

If it is a house that needs a major remodel or is not in rent-for-profit condition, get a renter that is really a caretaker. That is, rent the house for a nominal fee, like $50/month. This is a win-win situation since the tenant has a free or very cheap place to live and you have a caretaker at no cost. We tell our "renters" not to pay whatever nominal rent we have in the rental agreement. We both have a clear understanding that they are living there free, in exchange for looking after the property.

Not hiring a caretaker has 3 advantages:

1. No need to pay a caretaker

2. Not hiring an employee, which exposes you to potential labor issues

3. Easier to end a rental contract, than fire an employee

You do need to sign and notarize a rental agreement with your caretakers. Also, in the agreement, require the tenant to pay any utilities and other tenant-related bills. To get a fully enforceable rental contract, it should be registered with the Ministry of Housing.

We have never had a problem with a "renter" not vacating the premises when we ask. However, by registering the rental contract with the Ministry of Housing, they can enforce your request to vacate. Although, we have never registered our contracts with the Ministry of Housing, it is something to consider whether you are renting for profit or in exchange for caretaking the property.

Final Words

I don't recommend buying from anyone, expat or Panamanian, who has not done all the investigatory legwork I describe above. That is, unless you are willing to do all that legwork yourself – before you buy.

If you want to skip all that work and still buy ROP, you can safely do so by buying from someone, like us, who has done all that work for you.

Chapter 14

Not in Panama? How to Buy

»» ———————————— ««

Thankfully, you do not have to be in Panama to buy property in Panama. You may have found your property, done your due diligence, but due to competing demands in life, you cannot be on location to sign all the necessary purchase documents.

In that case, you can designate your lawyer, or someone else you trust, to have your Power of Attorney (POA). In Spanish a POA is refered to as a Poder. A Poder legally authorizes a designated person to sign the sale contract and related documents on your behalf.

POA Process - 3 Situations

The process to get a POA depends upon whether you are in the country or not and if you will buy the property via a corporation or in your own name. The 3 situations are listed below. Later in this chapter, I describe how to get a POA in each situation.

1. Buying property with your Panama corporation or foundation? No POA is needed.

2. You must grant someone your POA to buy the property while you are NOT in Panama.

3. While you were still in Panama, you are able to grant someone your POA to buy the property. If you can do this, it is a much simpler and faster process than doing the POA process from outside of Panama.

When Buying Property - Corporation

As I stated above, if the property you are buying will be held in a corporation or foundation, you do not need a POA to buy it.

Your lawyer can prepare and sign the purchase papers on behalf of your new entity (i.e., corporation or foundation). Your registered agent, typically your lawyer, can sign the purchase documents on behalf of the corporation. You will simply need to coordinate with your lawyer to get all documents and signatures done at the appropriate times.

Keep in mind, you can also grant your lawyer a POA so that he or she can create a corporation or foundation with which to buy a property. You can grant that POA while you are in Panama, or from another country, per the information provided below.

When Buying Property in Own Name

If you are buying a property in your own name and you are NOT in Panama, you need to grant someone in Panama your Power of Attorney to purchase the property. You have 2 ways you can do this from another country.

Apostille vs Authentication Process

To create a fully legal POA (or poder, in Spanish) while you are NOT in Panama, you must use 1 of the 2 options listed below.

Please Note: You can also use the apostille or authentication processes, described below, to certify public documents such as your marriage or birth certificate. You will need to certify such documents if you apply for a permanent resident visa.

- **Authentication process.** The authentication process requires that the POA be certified by the Panamanian Consulate. That is, by the Panamanian Consulate or Embassy located in your home country, specifically the one located closest to your home address. Subsequently, it must be processed by Panama's Ministry of Foreign Affairs, located in Panama.

- **Apostille process.** The apostille process is a simpler process. However, it is only available to the approximately 120 countries that are members of the Hague Convention of 1961. (Note: Canada is NOT a member of the Hague Convention. Use this link for a list of member countries: apostilleservices.com/hague-apostille-countries.)

The details of each of these 2 processes are explained below:

Authentication Process

The authentication process involves the 6 steps below:

1. You will need to have a hard copy of the Power of Attorney (POA) document, written in Spanish. Typically, your lawyer will provide this for you. The POA document should be printed on legal-sized paper. This is the preferred format in Panama.

2. You must sign the Power of Attorney document in front of a licensed Notary in your country. The stamp and signature of the notary should be clear and legible.

3. Next you must contact the Panamanian Consulate nearest to your home address to get your POA authenticated. The Consulate is responsible for verifying and certifying the document and the

corresponding signatures. The Consulate will attach the consul's signature to the document to certify its validity.

4. You can visit the Consulate in person or complete the process by mail. Typically, the Consulate requires the following items: 1) signed and notarized POA, 2) cashier check for the authentication service (~$30), 3) copy of your passport(s), and 4) self-addressed and stamped return envelope. Most Panamanian consulates in the USA recommend you use FedEx for this return service. I recommend calling or visiting the Consulate's website to verify their current authentication requirements. *If there is no Panamanian Consulate in your country, you can request authentication by a Panamanian Consulate located in a country friendly to Panama. For this purpose, a country is considered "friendly" to Panama if Panama has a consulate in that country AND that country has a consulate in Panama. The POA (or any document) must be authenticated in both of those Consulates. Subsequent to getting those certifications, you would then proceed to*

complete steps 5 and 6, below, of the authentication process.

5. Once the Consulate (or Consulates, if you have no Panama consulate in your country) returns the POA, now authenticated, you need to send the POA to Panama. You should send it to someone, probably your lawyer, who can do the next step in the process. (Note: The fastest way to send documents to and from Panama & the USA, in our experience, is DHL. Not cheap, but fast and reliable.)

6. Your lawyer, or whomever is the person you are granting the POA, then needs to submit the authenticated POA to the Department of Authentication and Legalization in the Ministry of Foreign Affairs. This department verifies the information provided by the Panamanian Consulate abroad, as well as the consul's signature, and then authorizes the foreign document for legal purposes in Panama.

At this point, your authenticated POA is valid and can be legally used in Panama.

A country, like Canada, that is not part of the Hague Convention MUST use the authentication process. However, even countries, like the USA, which are members of the Hague Convention can use the authentication process to legalize POAs and other documents.

Apostille Process

If you can use the apostille process, you should. It is a much easier and faster process. As I have mentioned, the apostille process is only available to the approximately 120 countries that are members of the Hague Convention. To find out if your country is a member of Hague Convention of 1961, visit this link: apostilleservices.com/hague-apostille-countries.

The apostille is an official certification that validates the origin of a public document and is issued in one nation to be used in another nation - where both nations are part of the Hague Convention of 1961. (FYI - Panama is a member of the Hague Convention of 1961.)

The apostille certifies that a competent authority has placed the signature and stamp on the document. This certification allows the document to have legal validity abroad. As a result, there is no need for Panama's Ministry of Foreign Affairs to further certify the document.

The 4 steps you need to follow to get your POA apostilled are listed below.

Note: if you need to get an apostille for a document like a marriage certificate, you only need to follow steps 3 and 4 below. I provide more details on getting an apostille on those types of public documents later in this section.

1. You will need to have a hard copy of the Power of Attorney (POA) document, written in Spanish. Typically, your lawyer will provide this for you. The POA document should be printed on legal-sized paper. This is the preferred format in Panama.

2. You must sign the Power of Attorney document in front of a licensed Notary in your country. The stamp and signature of the notary should be clear and legible.

3. Visit or mail your POA to the state department of your home state or province to request an

apostille. Typically, you will need to provide the signed and notarized POA, a copy of your passport(s), and payment for the service. Call your local state department or visit their website for their specific requirements and options.

4. Once the relevant State Department returns the apostilled POA, send it to the person to whom you granted a POA in Panama. Regarding POAs, typically the POA itself includes an expiration date, regardless of the apostille.

Apostille Process for Public Document

For other types of documents, such as a birth certificate, to get an apostille you need to mail the document to the state department of the issuing province or state. For example, if you were born in Oregon you should ask Oregon's State Department to apostille the certificate, even if you are currently living in New York. Likewise, documents issued at the national level, for instance your background check, will need to be apostilled by the Federal government's state department. Your local and national websites will provide detailed requirements to get an apostille from their respective state departments.

The apostille legalizes public documents that have been issued in another country, so that such documents can be used in Panama. Once apostilled, the documents in question can be used freely in any of the Hague Convention's member countries with no additional validations.

Keep in mind, that apostilles on permanent documents, such as a college degree or birth certificate, don't expire. However, apostilles on more temporary documents, such as a marriage certificate, do expire. Typically, such an apostille will be valid for 90 days to 6 months, depending upon the document. Regarding POAs, typically the POA itself should include an expiration date, regardless of the apostille.

Do POA While In Panama

The fastest and easiest way to grant someone your POA is to sign the POA document while you are still in Panama. If during your visit you found a property to buy, save yourself time and grief by signing a POA before you leave Panama.

You can grant anyone you trust your POA to sign your purchase contract: a friend, your lawyer, etc...

Below is the process to obtain a valid POA while in Panama:

1. Typically, you would have your Panamanian lawyer draft the POA to allow your selected proxy to sign all legal documents related to the purchase of the property. You can also have the staff at the Public Notary compose your POA, however, I don't recommend it. Not only is it very time consuming, but you have little control over the quality and accuracy of the document, especially if you are not fluent in Spanish.

2. Then, with your POA document in hand, you and your proxy need to visit a Public Notary in Panama to obtain the Notary's certifying stamp. You will also need to bring your IDs and cash (not a credit card) to pay for the service. It is best to use a Notary in a town of some size, like David. Public Notaries in smaller towns like Volcan or Puerto Armuelles, have limits to their authority. To ensure

your document won't have any issues, it is best to use a Public Notary in a larger town.

3. The Notary office will then issue you a valid POA that can be used by your proxy for the purchase of your property. You can pay extra to get additional "original" copies of the POA.

Copies and Register Your POA

Regardless of the process you used to obtain a valid POA, you should ensure that both you and your proxy have copies of the POA. In order for your proxy to sign for you, he or she must have a copy of the POA in hand to verify his or her authorization to sign the documents on your behalf.

You may also want to submit the POA to the Panama's Public Registry. That way even if all the copies are lost, the POA can be accessed and its existence verified both online and in person.

Final Words

I want to be quite clear; I do not recommend buying a property unless you have seen it in person. Ideally, you should spend enough time in the area to ensure it is truly where you want to live and invest, before purchasing a property. But if you cannot be in the country when it comes time to sign the necessary purchase agreement, it is good to know how to close the deal anyway.

Chapter 15

9 Steps to Protect Your Real Estate Investment

»» ———————————— ««

Protect Your Investment

Buying real estate in any foreign country can be stressful, especially when you do not speak the native language.

However, thousands of foreigners have successfully purchased property in Panama. By studying this guide, and hiring a good Panama real estate lawyer, you can protect yourself from getting scammed or buying real property with title defects or other problems.

9 Steps to Safeguard Your Purchase Process

To ensure you have no problems with your Panama real estate purchase, make sure you take these 9 steps:

1. Obtain a Title Report

The seller or real estate agent can provide you with the property's title number. If you go to Panama's Public Registry website (registro-publico.gob.pa) and search for that number you will uncover its Abstracts of Title ("Historias de la Fincas"). These Historias are written reports that show all the ownership changes for that specific real estate parcel or finca. The Historia includes the property's boundaries, area, and any encumbrances such as mortgages, liens, court orders, which could affect the property. Keep in mind, these reports are all in Spanish.

2. Get a Survey

Many property surveys, especially from the 1940s through the 1960s, were not very precise. That means the property boundaries recorded in the Public Registry for those properties may be in error.

For this reason, when buying land in Panama you may want to hire a surveyor to ensure that the purchase contract has the correct area and boundaries of the property.

Given that the previously recorded land area may be different from the newly performed survey, you may want to use a price per square meter in the purchase contract rather than a flat price. If you use the price per square meter method, then the property's total price can be modified to reflect the actual number of square meters being sold. To use that method, the due diligence period must be long enough to allow time to conduct a survey.

3. Title Before Making Full Payment

Some sellers may insist on being paid in full prior to transferring the title deed into the buyer's name.

That is a bad idea. Once the seller is paid in full, his motivation to record the deed is not nearly as strong.

When the seller insists on being paid first, one way to resolve this conflict is through a Panama bank's Promise to Pay letter. Such a letter guarantees the seller will be paid, after the title is transferred to the buyer. This is because the bank will be holding the buyer's final payment for the property.

Another way to accomplish this is to set up an escrow account with a reputable escrow company. The escrow company is required to pay the seller once the title is transferred to the buyer.

Only when the title is transferred to the buyer, free and clear of all encumbrances should the seller be paid in full.

4. Latent Hidden Defects

The Purchase Contract should contain a clause regarding "latent defects" allowing the buyer to cancel the contract if a hidden flaw or legal problem with the title is discovered.

5. Easements

Some properties have easements associated with them. An easement gives a third party the right to use the land for a specific benefit. Such a benefit could include an access road or path that allows a neighbor to access a property with no road access, or an easement may allow the public to access the beach. Utility companies and government agencies may have easements, as well.

Most easements can be found in the title report or title abstract. There are cases in which a legal easement exists but has not been formally filed with the Public Registry. This is why you should ask the neighbors about any easements that may impact the property you are interested in buying.

6. Double Titles

Rarely, a property may have 2 titles, each held by a different person or entity. Sometimes both titles are for the exact same property. More often, the property boundaries cited in each title simply overlap to some extent. Working together the surveyor and your lawyer should investigate any conflicting titles by contacting the public registry, owners of both titles, and the neighbors to resolve the conflitcting claims.

Local authorities such as, the municipality, the Agrarian Reform Directorate, and the Catastro, should also be contacted to find out if there are any competing claims regarding the title. In short, you need to find out if someone, other than the seller, has filed a title petition with one of these government agencies.

7. Real Property Taxes

Property taxes are collected by the Panama's revenue agency, Dirección General de Ingresos (DGI). If any back taxes are owed, the seller must pay them. A buyer needs to ensure that all back property taxes are fully paid before the title is transferred into his or her name.

8. Protecting Your Assets

For protection from future creditors or lawsuits, you may choose to buy a property using a corporation. For the ultimate protection, you should hold the property title in a Panama corporation whose shares are held by a Panama Private Interest Foundation. This ensures complete anonymity of ownership and provides double insulation from personal future creditors looking for assets that can be seized. Assets owned by such legal entities cannot be attached or seized. Such a structure also provides a cost effective method for Estate Planning and Probate avoidance so your heirs can receive your properties quickly and cheaply.

For more on the pros and cons, especially for US citizens who hold property in corporations, please read Chapter 6: Pros & Cons of Forming A Corporation.

9. Title Insurance

You can mitigate many, if not all, of the risks noted above by buying title insurance. Title insurance protects you from defects in the title, liens, encumbrances, double title, and property line problems. Although there are no Panama-based title companies, there are US title insurance companies that operate in Panama. These title companies offer the same types of title protection in Panama as they do in the US.

Chapter 16

Frequently Asked Questions

» ———————— «

In this section, I answer a number of commonly asked property-related questions. Most of which were not answered in the main body of this guide. Please feel free to contact me for clarification or to ask a question I have not answered. Use this shortlink (lynx2.co/slicecontact) to visit the contact page on my LivinginPanama.com website.

You may also want to explore the FAQs on my site, using this shortlink: lynx2.co/slicefaq. Those FAQs cover a wide range of topics related to living, investing and moving to Panama.

Is it legal for foreigners to buy Panama property?

Yes, buying property in Panama as a foreigner is both legal & safe. Thousands of foreigners own property in Panama. There are over a dozen laws in Panama established specifically for protecting foreign investments. In fact, private property is protected by Panama's constitution.

How long does it take to buy property?

The timeframe for buying property in Panama varies widely. We have purchased property in as little as 1 day. However, those purchases involved a simple contract for ROP property for which we paid cash.

Generally, from the time the Promise to Buy/Sell contract is signed to the closing, it can take anywhere from 15 days to 4 months. On average, it takes about 90 days for a titled property to close after the Promise contract is signed.

How to search for property in Panama?

The most efficient way to look for property is first to decide where and what type of property you are looking to buy. I talk about being clear on this in Chapter 1: Before You Look For Property. Once you know that you can start online. Some larger listing sites such as viviun.com and encuentra24.com and panama.craigslist.org, have listings from all over Panama. These sites also offer the ability to do a geographic search. In addition, there are other websites that only provide listings in a particular area or town in Panama. A few Google searches will reveal many of these real estate sites.

Keep in mind that not all Panama property for sale, especially property sold by locals, can be found online. That is why it is important to visit an area in which you are interested in living. First, you should visit before looking too hard for property simply to make sure you really do want to live there. And second, only by visiting can you discover all the properties that are for sale in that area.

How long does it take to register a title?

If you purchased a titled property, you must register or transfer the title into your name at the Public Registry. If you are willing to pay a fee to expedite the process, the entire registration can be done in as little as 2 business days. Typically, the process takes 1 to 3 weeks, depending upon how many other applications the Public Registry is working on.

Is title insurance available in Panama?

Title insurance is not generally offered by Insurance Companies in Panama. However, Panama has title insurance companies from the United States that offer the same services as in the US.

Title insurance protects real estate buyers by ensuring that the title has: no flaws, no competing ownership claims, no encumbrances, no boundary disputes, no liens, and no encroachments on the property. Title insurance in Panama typically costs about 1% of the sales price.

People buy title insurance because even the most thorough title search is not foolproof. There can be hidden title defects. These defects can include forgeries, fraud, seller's mental incompetency, defective deeds, undisclosed spouse, and clerical records errors. A defective title transfer or a hidden encumbrance or lien can result in the deed being challenged, or it can result in unexpected payments. Panama title insurance can cover all of these potential problems, thereby protecting your investment.

What are the closing costs and who pays them?

Generally, each party pays for their own closing costs. For example, sellers pay their attorney to draft the buy/sell contract, as well as the sales and capital gains tax, typically equalling 5% of the sale price.

Buyers pay their attorney for reviewing the buy/sell contract, doing the title search, title transfer, escrow services, as well as fees for the notary, public registry, updating the tax department records.

However, in some cases, buyers and sellers might negotiate terms dictate that the buyer or the seller pays all closing costs.

Are property appraisals available?

Although the government does not appraise properties for tax purposes, relying instead upon the registered or sales price, there are private appraisal companies in Panama. The following are considered by national banks to be reputable appraisal companies: AIR, AVINCO, Zubieta y Zubieta, Panamericana de Avaluos and Panama Florida, to name a few.

You can get a property appraisal for anywhere from $150 to $1000 or so. This depends upon the size, type, and location of the property.

How much do home inspections cost?

The cost of home inspections in Panama is typically between $150 to $300, depending upon the property and its location.

Is Rent-to-Own a purchase option in Panama?

Yes, rentals or leases with an option to purchase are legal in Panama. Keep in mind, all rental or lease contracts must be registered with the MIVI (Ministerio de Vivienda or Ministry of Housing) for them to be enforceable.

Can owners of Beachfront property block public access to the beach?

Panamanian law mandates public access to all beaches, oceans, lakes, and rivers in Panama. According to the law, unless there is access within 1000 meters from your property, you must allow public access.

In particular, regarding public access to beaches, the law considers that the public owns the first 22.5 meters from the median high tide mark. If you buy beachfront property and plan to build a structure that extends into the water (e.g. a pier or even an entire home on stilts above the water), you'll need to obtain a concession to do so.

The process to get a concession can take years, and no building permits can be obtained until it is granted. When buying property that already has structures in the public access area, you should verify that the proper concession has already been granted. (Note: this restriction only applies to the area in and immediately adjacent to the water. The rest of the land is yours to do with as you see fit.)

What is the justice system like in Panama?

In Panama you should do everything you can to stay out of court. Panamanian courts can be very unfriendly to foreigners and sometimes even corrupt. This is the main reason it's so important to do your due diligence before you buy.

As a Panama litigation lawyer explained to me: Panama does not have a justice system, rather it has a legal system. Unfortunately, the government's legal system and a fair and transparent system is not the same thing.

Is there Eminent Domain in Panama?

The Panamanian constitution states that the government cannot seize private property without just cause. Panama uses procedures similar to the eminent domain process in the US. And as in the US, if eminent domain is invoked in Panama, the property owner must receive fair market value for the land and any of its improvements.

What is the 10K rule?

The Panamanian constitution forbids property ownership by foreigners within 10 kilometers (6.3 miles) of the country's borders. You can read that article of the constitution below, first in Spanish, then in English.

"ARTICULO 291. Las personas naturales o jurídicas extranjeras y las nacionales cuyo capital sea extranjero, en todo o en parte, no podrán adquirir la propiedad de tierras nacionales o particulares situadas a menos de diez kilómetros de las fronteras."

"ARTICLE 291. Foreign natural or legal persons and nationals whose capital is foreign, in whole or in part, may not acquire ownership of national or private lands located less than ten kilometers from the borders."

This constitutional restriction is regulated and applied by the Public Registry, which regulates all titled land in Panama.

This means that foreigners cannot own land in their own name or in the name of a Panamanian corporation if that property is within 10 kilometers of the border.

You should always abide by the rules and laws of Panama. However, it is virtually impossible to enforce this rule for ROP property or for titled property that is held by a corporation in which all the directors are Panamanian.

In fact, many foreigners do own such land, titled and ROP, within 10 kilometers of the border. Surprisingly, often the title is held in their own name. So obviously, the enforcement of this stricture is not universal.

What liabilities apply to property flippers or investors?

Liability for real estate investors in Panama is limited. Taxes are the main liability. Upon each property sale, the seller must pay 2% transfer tax and 3% capital gains tax. If the property is held in a corporation, the seller instead needs to pay a 5% transfer fee. However, as long as the terms, conditions, and promises of the purchase contract are fulfilled, there are no other liabilities facing a real estate investor in Panama.

Can a 1031 exchange apply to Property in Panama?

Generally, no, a 1031 exchange is not applicable. That is, you cannot avoid paying US capital gains tax on a US property sale by reinvesting the proceeds in a property in Panama. This is because foreign property is not considered "Like-Kind" under the IRS code.

It may be possible to make use of a 1031 exchange if you sell a Panama property and then reinvest in another Panama property. However, such an exchange, if possible, would only be beneficial if you are on the hook for US capital gains tax on that property sale. For clarification, you should contact a US tax attorney for advice and guidance.

What is the process to obtain a building permit in Panama?

Your contractor, architect or engineer can obtain the necessary permits for you. Or, if you are your own contractor, you can have a sub-contractor obtain them for you. You can, of course, apply for a building permit yourself, but usually it is easiest if one of those individuals gets the permit (and sub-permits) for you.

Generally, this is because they know the process, the players, and they speak Spanish better than you do.

I will explain the permit process, in brief, below. However, you should do your own research to learn the specifics of getting a building permit in your area of Panama.

You need to get the following permits to build & then occupy your home:

- Temporary building permit, if needed (The request must be signed by a licensed contractor, architect, or engineer plus you need to provide proof of property ownership).
- Building, electrical, and plumbing permits
- Construction certificate
- Cutting and welding permit
- Then finally, Occupancy Permit. Note: the architect who signed off on the construction plans must also apply for the occupancy permit.

You need to provide the following to the appropriate authorities for approval:

- Architect, engineer, plumbing and septic, and electrical plans. These plans need to be stamped by a Panama licensed architect, civil engineer, plumber, and electrician respectively. None of these professionals are required to design these plans, but they must draw them up (in Spanish) and approve them by stamping the plans. Each of these plans must then be approved by the relevant agencies: Union Fenosa, IDAAN (water), MINSA (Ministerio de Salud), Bomberos (Fire Department), and the city engineer.

- Soil study and technical report (Only required for 2-story buildings)

- Copy of licenses for welder, electrician, plumber, etc.

- Survey of your property

- Copy of your passport

- Proof of ownership of the property

The timeframe and cost of getting a single building permit varies widely. Once you obtain the stamped plans, it can take anywhere from 1 week to several months to have your building permit approved.

How long this takes depends a lot upon the workload of the agencies needed for approval, the complexities of the plans, and the alignment of karma and the stars. Permit costs depend upon the value of your construction and where in Panama you are building.

What is the process & cost to create a housing development?

There are 6 steps in order to develop Panama real estate. That is, the steps required for segregating a large property into smaller residential lots for sale.

1. Have the property surveyed topographically by a Panamanian licensed surveryor.

2. Hire a licensed Panamanian architect to design or simply to draw up the master plan. It is required that a licensed architect draws the plan, even if that architect did not designed it.

3. Hire a Panamanian engineer to prepare the construction drawings. Again, the law requires that a licensed engineer do this.

4. Depending on the location and scope of the development, you will need a licensed Panamanian

environmental engineer to prepare an environmental impact study.

5. Submit the project for approval by ANAM (Autoridad Nacional del Ambiente). ANAM is the equivalent of the Environmental Protection Agency (EPA) in the US.

6. Submit the project to the local municipal engineer to get any needed construction permits.

The cost and timeframe to develop real estate in Panama depends on the location and scale of the project. Small projects can take only 3 months and cost only a few thousand dollars. Large-scale development projects can take years to obtain permits and can cost upwards of $50,000.

It really depends on the specifics of the project, where it is located, and the perceived impact it will have on the environment. Usually, once the environmental impact studies are approved by ANAM, the other municipal permits are relatively quick to obtain.

What is a concession?

A concession allows you to use land, such as National parks and beaches, which the government has removed from the real estate market. However, the government can grant a "concession" for the use of these lands.

Concessions are commonly granted for hotels and marinas that depend on such natural features to attract tourists and clients. However, concessions are frequently granted to individuals for personal residential use as well.

So, for example, if you plan on building a dock or a permanent rancho right on the beach you will need to obtain a concession. This is because the first 22.5 meters from the median high tide mark, on all Panama beaches, is set-aside for public access. If you obtain a concession, it is granted for either 20 or 40 years and is renewable.

However, due to backlogs these days, the concession approval process may take years. Unfortunately, you need a concession before you can apply for your building permit. The good news is that this concession only applies to the public access area. Therefore, you can build your house while you wait to get your concession request approved. Then, once it is approved, you can build your dock or waterfront rancho, or other structure that will intrude into the public access.

In reality, because of the long wait time, many people do go ahead and build their structures without approval. That is, of course, a risky course of action. In general, we suggest that you not build any structure or make any improvement on public property that you wouldn't mind losing.

When the concession is granted, it is given a registry number that is associated with the property. A concession is guaranteed by the government by means of a binding contract. Title insurance companies will generally offer title policies on a concession.

Is there zoning in Panama?

Zoning exists in Panama. Generally, most locations have setbacks and height restrictions, but some areas also restrict use or density. Panama City has the most intensive zoning restrictions, but other locations such as David and Boquete also have zoning use or density restrictions.

Panama's Ministry of Housing (MIVI) creates all of Panama's zoning classifications. If you go on their website you can find more information. At the time of this writing, MIV has online zoning maps and information for Panama City and David. See them on this link: miviot.gob.pa/index.php/ordenamiento-territorial.

So save yourself some time and money by learning if the property you want to purchase has been zoned. And, if so, what its zoning classification is. Specifically, you should make sure a property's zoning allows you to build the structure you want to build. You don't want to be slapped with a "Stop Work Order" for failing to comply with the zoning.

In our experience, many places in Panama lack strict zoning. This leads to an organic and co-mingling mix of residential, commercial, and industrials. This is much more the way the US was historically developed. There was a time when a blacksmith's shop, and a cabinetmaker's shop would have been built right alongside residences on a single block. In some ways, it's a lot more interesting this way. Many of the noise pollution issues of conflicting uses can be dealt with via noise ordinances, rather than with zoning restrictions.

Appendix

»» ———————————— ««

This appendix contains 3 topics that aren't specifically about buying property in Panama. However, they are likely to be of interest to people who want to buy property in Panama.

1. How to Pay Your Property Taxes in Panama
2. US Taxes & Panama Real Estate
3. Brief History - Land Ownership in Panama

How To Pay Your Property Taxes in Panama

»» ———————— ««

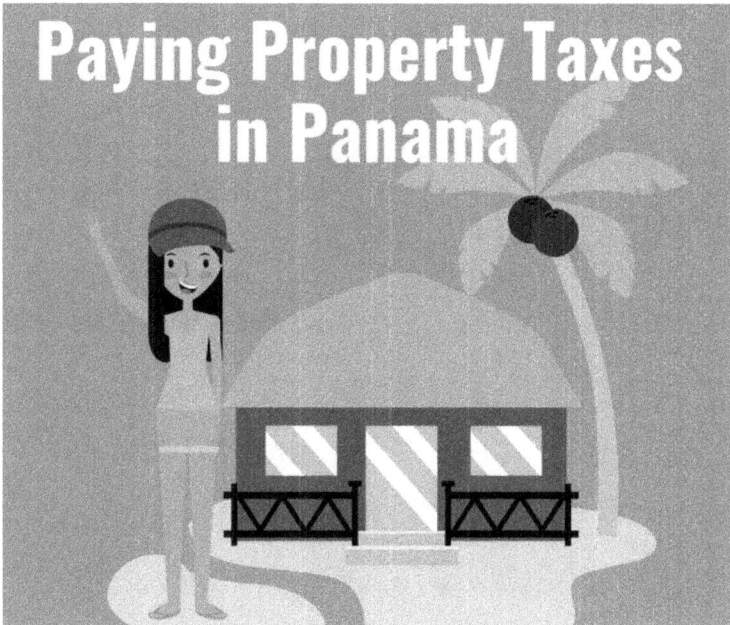

Paying Property Taxes in Panama

You will never get a bill or reminder to pay your Panama property taxes. It is up to you to remember to pay them – and on time! If you don't pay your property taxes, the government will collect them when you sell the property, plus penalties.

Below, I explain when and how to pay your Panama property taxes.

When to Pay & A Discount

Panama property taxes are paid in 3 installments, with these due dates:

- April 30th
- August 30th
- December 31st

Payments made after each due date will have a 10% surcharge.

You can get a 10% discount by paying your annual property taxes, in full, before March 1st.

Note: If you have a mortgage, the property tax payments will be collected by the bank in an escrow account.

Before You Pay

You need 2 numbers before you can pay your property taxes

1. **RUC - your property's tax ID number** (RUC - Registro Único de Contribuyente). It is not the same as your property's finca number. Every titled property in Panama is assigned its own RUC. The RUC is also your username when paying property taxes on the Department of Revenue's website. This department is called Dirección General de Ingresos (DGI).

2. **NIT - your taxpayer ID.** A NIT is your unique tax number. It is also used as your password on DGI's website. (NIT stands for número de identificación tributaria.)

How to get a NIT

If you do not have a NIT, then you need to request one at either of these two places:

1. Online at DGI's website (etax2.mef.gob.pa). There is no service charge to acquire a NIT or to use DGI's online system.

2. In person, by filling out the relevant form at a DGI office. It usually takes up to a week to approve and assign the NIT.

How Much To Pay

If you don't know how much property tax you owe, you can check the same DGI webpage (etax2.mef.gob.pa). You can also inquire at the DGI offices.

Where to Pay

Panama property taxes can be paid in 3 ways.

1. Visit a DGI office. You can pay with cashier's cheques, certified cheques, or credit cards (i.e., Visa, Mastercard or debit cards (Clave))

2. Pay at select banks such as: Caja de Ahorros, Banco Nacional, Banco General and Banvivienda. You will need your RUC and NIT numbers. Then you fill out the necessary form that is available at each of these banks. You can pay in cash or with a certified check made out to Tesoro Nacional.

3. Pay Online - Panama's tax department accepts online payment (etax2.mef.gob.pa). You will need to log into your personal tax account using your RUC (as your username) and NIT (as your password).

After you pay your tax, you should print your tax account statement, showing you have paid. You can also print certificates of good standing for property taxes (paz y salvos).

Keep Your Receipts

Always keep a file of receipts showing the tax payments you have paid, regardless of how you paid them. You may need to set the record straight when it comes time to sell the property.

US Taxes & Panama Real Estate

>> ———————————— <<

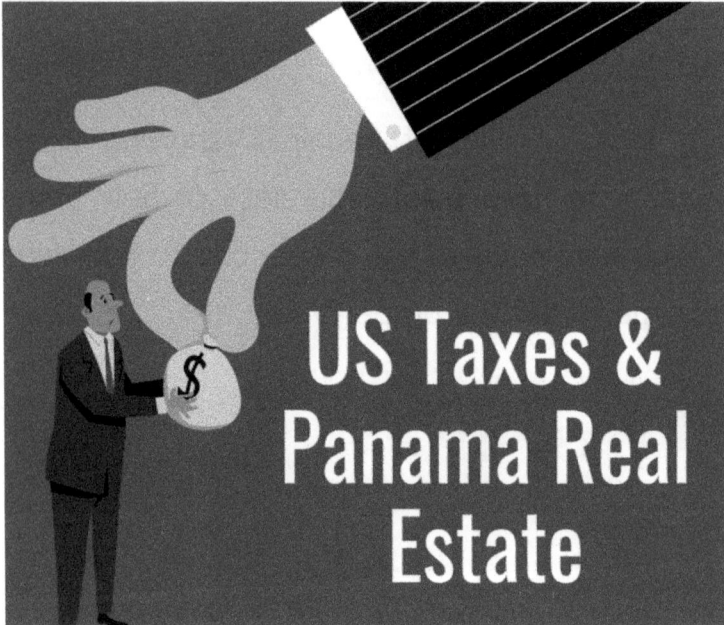

Before you buy or sell international real estate, you should think about the tax implications. This is true no matter your home country; however, I can only speak to the tax impact on US citizens.

Interestingly, one of the best ways Americans can save on taxes is by moving abroad.

By living overseas, US citizens can take advantage of the Foreign Earned Income Exclusion (FEIE), a special provision in the US tax code that allows US citizens living abroad to earn up to $107,600 (in 2020) - tax-free.

US Tax On Global Income

This is important because the US is one of only two countries in the world to tax its citizens on their worldwide income, including passive or investsment income. (The other country is the small African nation of Eritrea).

The US started taxing its citizens globally in 1861. They did it to help pay for the Civil War. Now, over 150 years later, it is still being enforced, and more stringently than ever.

Foreign Earned Income Exclusion (FEIE)

The FEIE provision allows qualifying citizens to legally evade paying US income tax on their first $107,600 (in 2020) of income or $215,200, if married and file jointly. And if you also qualify for the IRS's housing deduction or exclusion, you can save even more. In fact, these provisions can make moving to a lower taxation country very lucrative for Americans.

I go into more detail about the FEIE, the housing deduction, other taxes, deductions and loopholes, as well as US capital gains tax on sales of international real estate later in this section.

Foriegn Real Estate - An Invisible IRS Asset

There is another benefit to Americans who own international real estate. **That is, the IRS does not require, or even ask, taxpayers to report on their international real estate ownership.** The IRS does not consider the purchase of overseas property as a taxable event.

That is, until you convert the property to income by selling it. At that point, you may be liable to pay capital gains tax (see below), but before then the IRS has no interest in your overseas real estate. As you can imagine, the ability to keep mum on your international real estate porfolio can be helpful in a variety of situations.

Foriegn Taxes & US Federal Tax Credit

Before calculating your taxes, you need to know about the Federal Tax Credit. The purpose of this credit is for Americans to avoid double taxation. However, don't get too excited about this deduction, it in no way allows you to pay less in total taxes (US and foreign country taxes combined).

The IRS allows you to deduct or take a dollar-for-dollar credit for any taxes paid to a foreign country. In practice, this never works out perfectly, but it does eliminate most double taxes. The amount you can deduct depends upon the tax rate of the country where your land is located.

Capital Gains Tax

The sale of your foreign property can affect your US taxes more than any other activity. Therefore, below I give examples of the use of the Federal tax credit to calculate your capital gains tax.

Note: For the purpose of these examples, I assume a US long-term capital gain rate of 20%.

Capital gains tax of 33% (Columbia)

Say you bought a property in Medellin, Colombia in 2012 for $100,000. In 2020, you received an offer you couldn't refuse for $150,000, giving you a capital gain of $50,000. The capital gains tax rate in Colombia is 33%, so you pay $16,500 to Colombia.

Since Columbia's rate (33%) is so much higher than the US (20%), you wouldn't owe any tax to the US. In this case, you would report the sale on Schedule D of your US personal return and deduct or take a credit for the $16,500 you paid to Columbia on Form 1116. This would allow you to pay $0 to the IRS.

Capital gains tax of 10% (Panama)

Now let's say you sell a property in Panama. Panama's capital gains rate is 10%. In this case, you will pay 10% to Panama and 10% to the United States, to arrive at the US's 20% rate for long term capital gains.

Capital gains tax of 0% (Costa Rica & Ecuador)

If this same transaction took place in Costa Rica, where real estate sales are not taxed, you would pay the full 20% capital gains tax to the IRS in the US.

Important Note: When deciding in which country to buy real estate, that country's capital gains rate only comes into play if it exceeds the US rate. If a country's capital gains rate is 0% to 20%, you will pay 20% in total. If a country's rate is more than 20%, then only the excess should be considered in your decision. For example, Columbia's higher tax rate of 33%, means you will pay 13% more in capital gains tax than if that property had been in Panama or Costa Rica.

Also, while you may think you are saving money by buying and selling land in Costa Rica because they have no capital gains tax, this might not be the case. Costa Rica and other countries have other taxes and duties to make up for their zero capital gains rate. These taxes may not be deductible on your US return. In most cases, you are better off buying property in a country whose tax system is similar to the United States.

Foreign Earned Income Exclusion

As I mentioned, by living overseas, US citizens can take advantage of the Foreign Earned Income Exclusion (FEIE) to earn up to $107,600 per year (in 2020), tax-free.

That amount of the exclusion varies and is indexed to inflation. So for example, in 2017, the amount was $102,100. And in 2019, it was $105,900.

That means that as a US citizen living abroad, you can earn a little over $100,000 a year and not pay US taxes on it.

How To Qualify For FIEE

In order to qualify for the Foreign Earned Income Exclusion, you will need to prove to the IRS that your 'tax home' is in a foreign country.

The IRS uses two methods to assess whether you have a tax home abroad. So US citizens need to pass either one of two tests: 1) the physical presence test and 2) the bona fide residence test.

1. Physical Presence Test

In order to qualify under the physical presence test, you must be a US citizen who is physically present in one (or several foreign countries) for at least 330 days over the course of 12 consecutive months. However, the 330 days do not have to be consecutive.

That is, 330 full days. If you leave the US at 10am on a Tuesday, that day will not count towards your time abroad. To count, you must be outside the US for the entire 24 hours of each of those 330 days.

Consequently, to pass the physical presence test you can only be in the US for a total of 35 or 36 days a year.

That is the only test criteria. Other considerations like, why you are living overseas or what type of foriegn visa you have, does not matter. What matters is that you must not be in the US for 330 days or more over a 12 month-period.

2. Bona fide residence test

Thankfully, using the bona fide residence test, even if you spend more than 35 days in the US, you could still qualify for the Foreign Earned Income Exclusion.

To qualify under the bona fide residence test, you must demonstrate to the IRS that you have set up a home abroad; that you really have moved out of the US.

This is a subjective test. That is, the IRS needs to evaluate your situation to determine if you quality.

The IRS will look at various factors. For instance, do you have a local bank account, cell-phone contract or land phone? Do you rent or own a home abroad? Also whether you maintain a home in the US. (You are better off if you do not.) Also does your family live with you overseas. However, if you really do live abroad, you shouldn't have any trouble passing the test.

Note: you must meet the requirements for an entire 365- day tax year to qualify.

The good news is that under the bona fide residence qualifications, there are no stict restrictions on how much time you can spend in the US each year. (Although, generally 4 months max in the US is a good guideline to follow.) So if you want to spend more than 35 days in the US each year, you should try qualifying under the bona fide residence test.

If you meet either of these two tests, you are likely eligible for the Foreign Earned Income Exclusion.

Qualifying Income

The Foreign Earned Income Exclusion only applies to income that you actively work to earn. That is, wages and salaries, including self-employment income.

The key is that the income must be earned outside of the United States. If the work is done in the US, even if it is delivered to a foreign customer, it does not qualify for the FEIE. The work must be performed and delivered in a foreign country.

However, a US citizen who works for an American company could move abroad and seek to qualify for the Foreign Earned Income Exclusion because his work is performed overseas, even if it is for an American company.

Unearned passive income like dividends, capital gains, interest, and other types of income like social security and pension benefits are NOT included in this exclusion. You will need to pay your full tax bill on those. This includes any income you earn from the sale of overseas property.

Variable income like rents, royalties and other business profits are subject to individual consideration. Whether the income qualifies for the Foreign Earned Income Exclusion depends on your level of involvement with the business. Also, again, the income must be from overseas.

Keep in mind, if you are self-employed, you will still have to pay US self-employment tax, even if you qualify for the Foreign Earned Income Exclusion.

Overall, the Foreign Earned Income Exclusion means that if you qualify, you can exclude $105,900 of earned income from wages from your tax declaration during the year.

For example, if you live in Panama full-time and earn $200,000 per year, you may deduct $107,600 (in 2020) from your reportable income.

That means you'll pay tax on only $92,400 of the total $200,000.

If you are married, you and your spouse can BOTH qualify for the Foreign Earned Income Exclusion, meaning you'll be able to deduct a total of $215,200 from your income tax bill if you qualify and file jointly.

The IRS has an interactive tax assistant tool (irs.gov/help/ita) you can use to help determine if you qualify for the FEIE.

How To File For FIEE

Filing for the Foreign Earned Income Exclusion is straightforward.

When you file your 1040 income tax return you need to include form 2555. On form 2555, you will provide details about the income you earned in Panama (or other foreign countries).

The Big IRA Overseas Loophole

The FEIE is not the only way to pay less in US taxes. By purchasing Panama real estate using your retirement account, you can defer or eliminate US tax on both rental profits and capital gains.

The ability to leverage your retirement account, tax-free is one of the great offshore loopholes. This is often called using a self-directed IRA, which I explain in Chapter 8, Financing Your Purchase.

For instance, you may only have to pay the capital gains tax of the foreign county when you sell your property. In the case of Panama, that would result in a capital gains tax of only 10%.

Let me explain: If you move your IRA, or other type of retirement account, away from your current custodian and into a Panama corporation (or other offshore country corporation), you can invest that account in foreign real estate. Then the corporation is owned by your retirement account and holds investments on behalf of that account. You buy the rental property in the name of the corporation; pay its operating expenses from the corporation, and the profits flow back into the corporation and into your retirement account.

This only applies to investment rental real estate and not to property you personally occupy. If you later decide to live in the property, the funds must first be distributed out of the retirement account and any applicable taxes paid.

If you wish to purchase overseas real estate with funds from your IRA and a non-recourse loan, or you are in the active business of real estate, you can add a specially structured overseas corporation to eliminate US tax.

If you buy real estate with an IRA in the United States, you get the joy of paying tax on the gain attributed to the money you borrow (the mortgage). If 50% of the purchase price comes from your 401K and 50% from a loan, half of the rental profits and half of the gain is taxable, with the other half flowing into your retirement account.

Perform this same transaction overseas, and no US tax is due.

Foriegn Real Estate & Depreciation

Owners of rental real estate in the United States can use accelerated depreciation to deduct the value of property over 27.5 years. However, if the property is overseas, a straight-line depreciation must be used over 40 years. The straight-line method gives you less bang for your depreciation buck.

This means that on a $100,000 rental property, your annual depreciation deduction would be about $3,636 for a US property vs. $2,500 for a property in Panama. So you would pay a premium of $1,136 on the overseas property.

It may sound like an issue, but it isn't necessarily. A straight-line depreciation can also save you money. Accelerated depreciation is great if you plan to hold the property for about 20 years. However, if you plan to buy, improve and then sell over a short period (a few years), then accelerated depreciation will cost you money, not save you money.

This is because depreciation is "recaptured" when you sell the property. Every dollar you were allowed to deduct over the years must now be paid back. It is added to your basis, and taxed at 25% rather than 20%. So, as a rough example, if you have a gain of $50,000 and took depreciation of $20,000, you owe tax at 20% of $50,000 for $10,000 plus 25% of $20,000 for $5,000. Therefore, your total tax due is $15,000.

The more depreciation you take, the more you must repay. If you hold a property for many years, taking a deduction today, and paying it back in the distant future, is a benefit. If you will sell the property in 3 or 5 years, taking the deduction now, and paying an additional 5% in tax later, is of little to no benefit.

This might lead some to think a good strategy is to not take depreciation, especially on property you plan to quickly flip. Well, the IRS has a surprise for you: The tax law requires depreciation recapture to be calculated on depreciation that was "allowed or allowable". This means you will pay tax on depreciation whether you take it or not.

All of this is to say that not being allowed accelerated depreciation on offshore real estate might be a good thing.

Primary Residence Exclusion & Foriegn Real Estate

Remember, all of the same US tax rules apply to Panama real estate (and all overseas property) that apply to US properties. This includes the primary residence exclusion. Therfore, if you qualify, you can exclude up to $250,000, if single, or $500,000, if married and filing jointly, from the sale of your primary residence.

To qualify, you must own and occupy the home as your principal residence for at least two years of the last 5 years before you sell it. This applies whether your home is a house, apartment, condominium, or even a mobile home.

To get the $500,000 exclusion, both a husband and wife must live in the home as their primary residence. It is possible for one spouse to qualify while the other does not. This would occur if a husband is living in the United States and only occasionally visits his wife and family in Panama. In that case, in a joint return, only the wife may take the exclusion for $250,000 when they sell their home in Panama.

You don't need to spend every minute in your home for it to be your principal residence. Short absences are permitted. For example, you can take a two-month vacation and count that time as part of the 2 years. However, long absences are not permitted. For example, if you are away from home for a whole year you cannot count that year as one of the 2 years.

Like-Kind/1031 Exchange & Foreign Property

Because you get the "benefit" of all US tax rules when it comes to overseas real estate, you can use like-kind exchanges (also called a Section 1031 exchange) to defer US tax.

There is one big exception. You can't exchange US property for foreign property or vs versa. You can only exchange a foreign property for foreign property.

In a like-kind exchange, you defer paying taxes by buying, with the proceeds from the sale, a similar property owned by someone else. The property you buy is treated as if it were a continuation of the property you gave up. The benefit is that you defer paying taxes on any profit you may have received.

All real estate owned for investment or business use outside of the United States is considered to be like-kind with all other such real estate outside of the United States. Therefore, you can exchange an office building in Panama City, Panama, for an apartment building in Medellin, Colombia. However, as I have explained, you may not exchange a property in Panama with a property in New York.

Rental Properties & US Taxes

Rental income and expenses from overseas real estate is reported on your personal return, just as a US rental property would be. You must follow all US tax rules for deductions and expenses, such as depreciating improvements and deducting repairs.

Remember, you need to keep your receipts in case of an audit. This includes receipts for services you pay for in cash. Paying in cash is very common in Panama and other Latin American countries. A potential audit is yet another reason to get and keep receipts for all payments, especially for cash payments to contrators and other workers.

Regarding travel and other expenses associated with visiting your property, there are limits. If you are flying to Panama five times a year, hanging out for a week, and then expensing these trips against your one or two rental units, the deduction will not survive an audit. However, you most likely can expense one trip a year. If you have a more extensive overseas real estate porfolio, you can justify expensing more frequent trips.

When reporting your rental property, remember to take depreciation. As stated earlier, the only difference in offshore real estate is the allowed depreciation method. You must use a straight-line depreciation over 40 years.

US Tax Filing Obligations for Overseas Real Estate

Your overseas real estate will likely also require you to file a number of new US tax forms. The forms are not onerous, but if you don't file them you face substantial penalties if you are caught. These significant penalties are aimed at punishing Americans who are hiding money offshore, but they could ensnare you as well.

FBAR

The most critical IRS tax form to remember to file is the FBAR (aka, the Report of Foreign Bank and Financial Accounts, Form TD F 90-22.1). Anyone who is a signor or beneficial owner of a foreign bank or brokerage account (or combination of accounts) with a value of more than $10,000 must disclose their account(s) to the US Treasury.

This means, if you had $10,000 in foreign bank account (or a combination of accounts), even for a day, you must report that account(s) in your taxes and also file an FBAR form.

That is, on your tax return you will be asked if you had an account with $10,000 or more. It is simple yes or no question. But that is not the end of it. You still need to file the FBAR.

The FBAR is a separate form. And you don't send it to the IRS, you send it to the US Treasury Department.

FBAR Due Date

Thankfully, the FBAR due date is now April 15th, with an automatic extension of 2 months for US citizens living abroad. (Prior to 2016, the FBAR due date was June 30th). Also an extension is now available, which if you request it, moves the FBAR due date to October 15th.

Other Required IRS Forms

You are also required to file IRS form 5471 if you own a foreign corporaton, even if the corporation contains zero assets or value.

Other tax forms may be required if you hold your property in a foreign corporation, foundation, or international trust.

Overseas Real Estate Professional Benefits & Definition

If you are working in real estate while living overseas, you can realize some great tax benefits. This applies to people who spend a significant amount of time and effort working in foriegn real estate. It does not apply to people with only one or two apartment units.

Typically, an investor in overseas real estate may only deduct losses against other passive income. If you do not have any other passive income that year, the losses are carried forward until you can use them.

The IRS allows exceptions to the above rule to participants in the management of overseas real estate. The IRS has 2 classifications for this exception:

1) active participants and 2) material participants in the management of foreign real estate.

As an active participant in offshore real estate, you can deduct up to $25,000 of passive losses against other income (like wages, self-employment, interest, and dividends) on your US tax return. This allowance is phased out on a 50% ratio if your adjusted gross income (AGI) is $100,000 or more.

However, if you can meet the material participant criterion, you will find that there are major international tax breaks and loopholes.

As a material participant you can deduct your expenses against any and all of your other income, regardless of source, without limitation or AGI phase-out.

While it is relatively easy to qualify as an active participant, it is far more challenging to be classified as a material participant in overseas real estate.

A material participant is sometimes referred to as a real estate professional. A material participant is much more involved and in control of real estate activities than an active participant. In order to materially participate in offshore real estate, you are most likely living and working abroad. For instance, it would be hard to qualify as materially involved in real estate in Panama while living in Texas.

Given that, material participants would most likely qualify for the Foreign Earned Income Exclusion (FEIE) as well. And when the FEIE is combined with your eligible overseas real estate business, you can take out a salary from that business, free of Federal income tax and make use of a number of other tax mitigation strategies.

Amnesty or Catching Up with US Taxes

If, after reading this chapter, you realize you have not been filing the required FBAR or other forms, or have not done your taxes correctly (or at all); no worries.

The IRS has an amnesty program with no penalties, if you voluntarily correct your past errors or omissions. However, you need to correct those errors and omissions before the IRS discovers them. Otherwise you will be heavily penalized.

Final Words

For most Americans, filing your US taxes while living overseas is no more difficult than it is if you live in the USA. However, there are some loopholes, exclusions, tax accounting, and tax forms you should be aware of as an American living abroad, especially when it comes to overseas real estate.

Brief History - Land Ownership in Panama

»» ———————————— ««

Panama Land - A History

In the beginning, land in Panama did not belong to anyone. The indigenous people used land collaboratively and communally.

Spanish Crown Owns It All

Then the Spanish came.

They declared all land in Panama belonged to the Spanish Crown. However, the Crown was only interested in using the land along the west coast, from Colon to Panama City. This oceanfront slice of land was of interest to the Crown for the same reason it is valuable now: as a profitable port for global trade.

Communal & Titled Land

In the interior, the Crown continued the communal tradition of Panama's indigenous people. They sold some land to villages to be owned collectively. However, they also granted some large tracts of land to a few of their favored subjects. On the remaining land, the Crown recognized the right of small farmers to use, but not to own, the land they farmed.

At that point in time, land in Panama was treated somewhat like it was in feudal England. That is, the Crown was fine with you using its land as long as you played nice and obeyed the King or Queen.

Keep in mind that even after the Crown's land grants and sales, the Crown technically owned almost all of the land in Panama. Which means, in today's terms, most of the land was ROP, with the Crown holding the title.

Panama Independence

Then, 300 years later, Spain left. At that point, all of the Crown's land belonged to the new Panamanian government.

Titling Encouraged, People Reluctant

The new Panama government asked its citizens to title any land they were using. All the government asked is that the property owners (or occupants) show some kind of proof that they had been using or living on the land. But very few people bothered to do that. For the most part, people saw no need to formalize or prove they were the owners of their property. It had been working fine as it was for the last 300 years.

General Omar Torrijos - Agrarian Land Reform

Then around 1968, General Omar Torrijos, implemented an agrarian land reform. His land reform included a way for people to "live on government land and work it in order to have the right to possess it". This strengthened and expanded the inventory of ROP property in Panama. General Torrijos' military regime spanned from 1968 to 1981.

Expense, Process & Taxes Discourage Titling

Although, the government has always vaguely encouraged peole to title their ROP land, not many people took that step. Getting title was an expensive and long process. Even many wealthy landowners didn't title their property.

Not only was the process onerous, but also once you titled the land, you were on the hook for paying property taxes. Plus you then had to pay capital gains taxes when you sold your titled property.

Most Land Still ROP in Panama

Today, titling is much cheaper, although not much faster.

But still, most land in Panama continues to be ROP, with the government holding the title. In many ways land ownership is similar to the way it was when Panama was a colony of Spain.

More Encouragement to Title

Recently, the Panama government has taken concrete steps to encourage property owners to title their land. The biggest step was the 2019 property tax reform. That bill made property valued up to $120k fully exempt from property taxes. Previously, only properties valued up to $30k were fully exempt.

Historically, many people don't want to title their land because they don't want to pay property taxes. Consequently, the government eliminated that reason by creating the new and higher property tax exemption.

Since most property in Panama is valued under $120k, the new exemption means that most property in Panama is now exempt from property taxes.

Unfortunately, is it is still takes a very long time to title property in Panama. The long processing timeframe is mostly due to the amount of time a title application sits undisturbed in various officials' inboxes.

Perhaps the government's next steps will be to decrease the cost and especially the length of time it takes to title land. Perhaps, over the next decade or two, most land in Panama could be titled, not ROP. Only time will tell.

About the Author

»» ———————— ««

Betsy Czark has spent much of the last 14 years in Panama – living, investing and writing about it. Her life in Panama started when Betsy, her husband Reyn, and their then 5 year old daughter, Skylar, spent 3 months exploring Panama by bus and taxi.

During that journey, they stumbled upon the charming beach town of Puerto Armuelles. It was love at first sight. They bought a house and settled in.

Betsy and Reyn also began to purchase property, learning significantly along the way. In this guide, she happily shares those lessons.

You can contact Betsy and learn more about Panama, on her website, LivinginPanama.com. :)